John C. Howell, a nationally respected trial lawyer, was admitted to the Florida Bar in 1955 and to the Colorado Bar in 1970. He has also been admitted to practice before all federal and state courts in those states, including the United States Supreme Court. A graduate of the University of Miami Law School, Mr. Howell has practiced extensively in corporate law. He is now a member or former member of the American Bar Association, the Federation of Insurance Counsel, the Legal Research Institute, and the American Arbitration Association. Author of a number of law review articles, Mr. Howell has also published sixteen books to date.

THE COMPLETE CITIZEN'S LAW LIBRARY

John C. Howell

PREPARE YOUR OWN PARTNERSHIP AGREEMENTS

How to form limited partnerships
Dissolve partnerships with
sample agreements and custom clauses
for special situations

A SPECTRUM BOOK

Prentice-Hall, Inc., Englewood Cliffs, New Jersey 07632

Library of Congress Cataloging in Publication Data
HOWELL, JOHN COTTON, 1926-
    Prepare your own partnership agreements.

    (A Spectrum Book)
    Edition for 1979 published under title: How
to prepare your own partnership agreements.
       1. Partnership—United States—Popular works.
I. Title.
KF1375.Z9H69 1980   346.73'0682   80-17243
ISBN 0-13-697235-7 (pbk.)

This publication is designed to provide accurate and authoritative information in regard to the subject matter covered. It is sold with the understanding that the publisher is not engaged in rendering legal, accounting or other professional service. If legal advice or other expert assistance is required, the services of a competent professional person should be sought.

—From a Declaration of Principles jointly adopted by a Committee of the American Bar Association and a Committee of Publishers.

For the purposes of editorial simplification, this publication generally uses the masculine pronoun in the generic sense, to indicate *person*. The author and the publisher are fully aware that the information in this volume pertains to women as well as men, and no discrimination is implied or intended.

PRENTICE-HALL INTERNATIONAL, INC., *London*
PRENTICE-HALL OF AUSTRALIA PTY. LIMITED, *Sydney*
PRENTICE-HALL OF CANADA, LTD., *Toronto*
PRENTICE-HALL OF INDIA PRIVATE LIMITED, *New Delhi*
PRENTICE-HALL OF JAPAN, INC., *Tokyo*
PRENTICE-HALL OF SOUTHEAST ASIA PTE. LTD., *Singapore*
WHITEHALL BOOKS LIMITED, *Wellington, New Zealand*

Contents

SAMPLE PARTNERSHIP AGREEMENT
FORMS

Preface

If you are one of the many people considering the formation of a business partnership this book will give you all the information you need.

It is very easy and inexpensive to establish a partnership. In fact, it can be done with nothing more than a handshake and a vague, general understanding that the partners will work together in a business venture with the hope and expectation of making money. However, the ease of entering into a partnership should not mislead you. There can be unexpected consequences. Serious legal responsibilities and liabilities are involved in becoming a partner in any business organization. The fact that you may have full and complete trust and confidence in your partner does not safeguard you from legal liabilities. I will warn you about these potential liabilities you assume as a partner.

Knowing about the liabilities of partnerships is important but you should also know your partners. No matter how well you know your prospective partner or partners, no matter how honest and understanding they may be, you should prepare your agreement in a business like way at the outset to avoid misunderstandings and legal entanglements later.

You have here all the basic forms as well as a complete checklist of items to consider in preparing your agreement. A partnership is not only a legal relationship, it is also a personal relationship or status. Before entering upon a partner relationship, the people involved generally should consider the advantages and disadvantages of this type of business organization as compared to those of the corporation or others. You'll find that information in this book.

Benjamin Franklin once said:

Partnerships often finish in quarrels; but I was happy in this, that mine were all carried on and ended amicably, owing I think, a good deal to the precaution of having very explicitly settled in our articles everything to be done by, or expected from each partner, so there was nothing to dispute, which precaution I would therefore recommend to all who enter into partnerships.

Introduction

The Uniform Partnership Act defines a partnership as "an association of two or more persons to carry on as coowners a business for profit." My definition is:

> A partnership is a contract of two or more competent persons to place their money, effects, labor, and skill in lawful commerce or business, and to divide the profit and bear the loss in certain proportions; it is a contractual relationship between individuals in which the members ordinarily possess the power to do, in business, what individuals can and usually do in such business, except as specifically limited by the partnership contract or denied by law.

To state that partners are coowners of a business means each has the power of ultimate control.

To determine if a particular association is a partnership, the test is whether the parties, acting in good faith and with a business purpose, intend to join together to conduct the enterprise. All the facts must be considered: the agreement, the conduct of the parties in carrying out its provisions, their statements, the testimony of disinterested persons, the relationship of the parties, their respective abilities and capital contributions, the sharing of profits and losses, the actual control of the business, and any other facts highlighting the true intent of the parties. When employed, this test presents a difficult problem particularly if the parties want to share the profits but not the losses, or if they want to share the income but not the control.

Frequently, people want the benefits of a partnership—but not the liabilities. In the development of the laws of partnership in England from 1600 to 1850 it was held that the receipt by a person of a share of the profits of the business was enough to make him a partner; but this objective test, easy to apply, was soon rejected as unworkable. Sharing profits is, indeed, a very important factor. For example, the Uniform Partnership Act provides that it is prima facie evidence that the person receiving a share of the profits is a partner in the business except where the profits are received as payment for a debt, wages, rent, annuity to a widow or representative of a deceased partner, interest on a loan, or as the consideration for the sale of good will.

On the other hand, a *limited partnership* is one in which the liability of some members, but not all, is limited. Such a partnership may be formed under most state statutes which permit an individual to contribute a specific sum of money to the capital of the partnership and limit his liability for losses to that amount. The partnership must otherwise comply with the requirements of the statute.

The formation of a partnership, the addition of a new partner to an existing partnership, and the making of contributions to an existing partnership may be accomplished without present tax consequences. Under the Federal Tax Code no gain or loss is recognized to the partnership or to any of its partners in the case of a contribution of property in exchange for an interest in the partnership. The contributing partner's basis for his partnership interest is the amount of money plus the adjusted basis of any property contributed. Property contributed to a partnership has the same basis which it had in the hands of the contributing partner at the time of the contribution.

One of the most difficult problems of partnership taxation is the treatment of the gain to the partner on the sale of his partnership interest. In general he is deemed to have disposed of a capital asset. However, in order to prevent tax avoidance, the Code adopts a special rule where the assets consist of unrealized receivables or substantially appreciated inventory, a part of which is attributed to the selling partner as ordinary income.

If you're interested in partnership investments as tax shelters, review the Tax Reform Act of 1976. The "partnership at risk" rule (Section 704[d]) which limits the losses allowed to a partner to the adjusted losses of his partnership interest, was amended by the Act of 1976 to provide:

For purposes of this subsection, the adjusted basis of any partner's interest in the partnership shall not include any portion of any partnership liability with respect to which the partner has no personal liability. The preceding sentence shall not apply with respect to any activity to the extent that Section 465 (relating to limiting deductions to amounts at risk in case of certain activities) applies, nor shall it apply to any partnership the principal activity of which is investing in real property (other than mineral property).

Activities to which Section 465 (Tax Reform Act of 1976) applies are:

1. holding, producing, or distributing motion picture films or video tapes,
2. farming (as defined in Section 464[e]),
3. leasing any Section 1245 property (as defined in Section 1245[a][3]), or
4. exploring for, or exploiting, oil and gas resources as a trade or business or for the production of income.

To the extent that many "tax shelters," in addition to real estate, are still available for investors, the partnership form of business organization may yield to other business entitles for tax purposes in the future.

For income tax purposes, the term "partnership" includes a syndicate, group, pool, joint venture, or other unincorporated organization through or by means of which any business, financial operation, or venture is carried on, and which is not a corporation or a trust or estate. This definition obviously expands the meaning of partnership under the definitions given above (but only for "tax" purposes).

A partnership as an entity is not subject to the income tax. It must file an annual return stating specifically the items of its gross income and allowable deductions, but this return is for information purposes only and no payment is required. In general, the taxable income of a partnership is computed in the same manner as in the case of an individual, except that income and loss must be itemized according to derivation, and except that certain deductions are not allowed.

The individual partners are liable for the payment of income tax. Each partner reports the tax due on his share of partnership income on his or her own individual return. A partner's share of partnership income is generally determined by the partnership agreement.

A *family partnership* is one whose members are closely related by blood or marriage. Family partnerships are sometimes created to shift income from the organizer of a business to members of his or her family. This reduces the family taxes if the family members are in lower tax brackets. Although tax savings is sometimes the only motive for the partnership, the Internal Revenue Service will recognize the arrangement if, after IRS investigation, the family members are found to actually own their partnership interests. This depends on the intent of the parties, determined from all the facts—the agreement, the relationship of the parties, their conduct, statements, individual abilities and capital contributions, who controls the income and how it is used, and any other facts showing their true intent.

The family partnership is frequently used where capital is a material income-producing factor, for example, the firm which requires large inventories or investments in plant and equipment. The Internal Revenue Service will recognize the family member if he or she actually owns a capital interest (even if he or she got it from another family member), provided the transaction vested him or her with dominion and control.

The donor may retain substantial powers as managing partner if other facts show that he or she really gave up part of his interest and made the donee its true owner. In the family partnership where the business income is primarily from fees, commissions, or other pay for personal services, the Internal Revenue Service generally will not recognize the family member unless he or she contributes substantial or necessary services.

In your consideration of a partnership as a business entity you should keep in mind that you are exposed to personal liability in all business transactions. Knowing this you should be very careful in the selection of your partners. In tax matters the question of whether a partnership exists will depend on the definitions set out in the Internal Revenue Code.

1

The Laws of Partnership

Historical Background of Partnership Laws

The business relationship known as partnership already existed when the Code of Hammurabi and the Mosaic law were being formulated. Partnership law today rests, in part, on the common law, but was developed in England from the civil law and from the law merchant. Partnership matters were decided in special mercantile courts, such as the Courts of Staple which received parliamentary sanction in England in 1353. But it was not until the middle of the eighteenth century, under Lord Mansfield, that the common law began to develop its commercial law. Although the use of the partnership form of business organization became widespread in the nineteenth century, there was considerable confusion as to the applicable law, which was a combination of the law merchant and the common law.

Prior to the development of the common law of England the law merchant or "The Law of Merchants" had a profound influence on the laws of partnership. The law merchant has been described as follows:

7

It may be defined as a number of usages, each of which exist among merchants and persons engaged in mercantile transactions, not only in one particular country, but throughout the civilized world, and each of which has acquired such notoriety, not only amongst those persons, but also in the mercantile world at large, that the Courts of this country will take judicial notice of it. A usage of the law merchant has therefore two characteristics—it must in the first place amount to jus gentium, that is to say, it must be in vogue beyond the limits of this country and its notoriety must be cosmopolitan rather than national; and in the second place it must be of such a nature that it will receive judicial notice in our Courts. It does not follow, however, that every mercantile usage of which the Courts take judicial notice forms part of the law merchant. It is composed of those usages of merchants and traders in the different departments of trade which have been ratified by the decisions of Courts of law and adopted as settled law with a view to the interests of trade and the public convenience. [X. Halsbury's *Laws of England,* 2d ed., 1933.]

In England, the Partnership Act of 1890 was enacted to codify the existing law on the subject while in the United States attempts were made in several states to codify the law on partnership.

The Uniform Partnership Act

The Uniform Partnership Act was approved in 1914 by the National Conference of Commissioners on Uniform State Laws. By 1980 the Uniform Act had been adopted in 48 states as well as in the District of Columbia and the Virgin Islands. Louisiana and Georgia are the

8

two states that have not yet adopted the Uniform Act. The basic purpose of the Uniform Act is to draft statutes governing the commercial law in clear, simple terms that can be utilized by all of the states. This will promote uniformity and stability in business law. Where the Uniform Act has been adopted, partnership cases decided under the common law prior to its adoption are of little assistance as precedents for cases which are controlled by the new statutory enactments.

Although the Uniform Act was primarily intended to codify existing statutory and common law, its enactment did bring about certain changes in the law previously in force. For instance, the Act affected the rules governing the acquisition and conveyance of real estate in the partnership name, the character of a partner's property as personal property, the nature of the liability of an incoming partner, the dissolution of partnerships, and the rights of creditors after the admission or retirement of a partner.

The Uniform Act makes new rules in some areas, such as in the provision for regulating the priorities for liability of a partner's interest, and for new property status called tenancy in partnership. (See Joint and Common Ownership of Property.) The Act does not contain all the law affecting partnerships. The question of capacity to become partners is generally decided on common law principles. Suits by and against partnerships in the firm name and service of process are generally subjects of special statutory regulations. Although most of the state statutes are patterned after this Act, they are not all identical. Therefore, when you have a specific question, check the wording of your state statutes. Limited partnerships, discussed later, are the subject of another uniform act.

Definition and Description of Partnerships

The widely accepted definition of a partnership is, according to the Uniform Partnership Act, "an association of two or more persons to carry on as coowners a business for profit." Draftsmen of the Uniform Act recognized that it is neither practical nor feasible to frame an exact and comprehensive definition of a partnership. This is partly because partnerships resemble and have certain features or characteristics in common with, various other groups, associations, transactions, or relationships. These distinctions are explained later to give you an understanding of the many situations in which you could unknowingly become a partner.

A more inclusive definition, based upon the historical development of partnerships, is that a partnership is a contract, express or implied, between two or more competent persons to place their money, effects, labor, or skill, or some or all of them, into business, and to divide the profits and bear the losses in certain proportions. As we shall see, these definitions can be better understood and more easily applied when we recognize the essential criteria, tests, or indicia of partnerships.

When the courts are presented with the question as to whether a partnership exists in specific fact situations, they generally look for four essentials.

1. Two or more parties intending to be partners
2. Sharing of profits and losses
3. Joint ownership and control of capital assets or property of the group
4. Joint control and management of the business (See Tests or Indicia of Partnerships.)

The two main types of partnerships are general and limited. *General partnerships* are further classified in some states as trading, or commercial, partnerships, and nontrading, or ordinary, partnerships. A limited partnership can be formed only by compliance with the statutory requirements.

A *trading partnership* is one engaged in the business of buying or selling for profit; any other partnership business is called a nontrading partnership. *Nontrading partnerships* include business or professional activities among attorneys, physicians, contractors, builders, farmers, plumbers, real estate brokers, insurance agents, and other service businesses or professions. Recent statutory enactments in some states authorize certain professional groups to form special professional corporations. These professional corporations are not partnerships. You should not attempt to form these without professional advice.

A *dormant partner,* also known as a secret or silent partner, is generally one whose name is not used by the firm, and who is generally unknown to those dealing with the partnership. This is a person whose connection with the partnership business is concealed and does not usually take any active part in the business. Silent partners have the same general powers as ordinary partners and have the same right to act for the firm in partnership transactions in the absence of stipulations to the contrary. Therefore, such a partner may be liable for firm obligations as are other general partners.

The terms *junior partner* and *senior partner,* while frequently used in law firms and other professional partnerships, have no special legal significance other than that which may be given to the terms in the specific partnership agreement. That occurs where in some states it is permissible for the partners, by written agreement, to establish the rights, powers, and duties of the junior partners as distinguished from the senior partners. Also, the agreement may provide for the varying rights and duties of nonpartner employees, such as associates, nonpartner members, and others.

Where a written agreement between the so-called junior partner and the firm does not give the junior partner the right of part ownership of the business (which is an indispensable requirement under the Uniform Act), he has been held by some courts not to be a partner. But there have also been some decisions to the effect that a junior partner, who has little or no voice in the management of the firm, may be liable for the losses of the partnership as any other partner. This question will, of course, depend primarily upon the particular facts and circumstances of each case. The written agreement should plainly state the status and responsibilities of each partner to avoid confusion and uncertainty.

Partnership as a Separate Entity

The adoption of the Uniform Partnership Act did not, as might have been expected, resolve the question as to the true nature of a partnership. An attempt was made in the early drafts of the Act to define a partnership as "a legal person formed by the association of two or more individuals for the purpose of carrying on a business with a view to profit." The final draft of the Act left the entity question unanswered. And the question has not yet been fully resolved.

Therefore, the various definitions of partnership do not clearly answer the question whether a partnership is a legal entity. Legal entity means a being or artificial person recognized by law as having rights, powers, and duties distinct from the individual persons making up such entity. While a corporation is recognized as a separate, legal entity for most purposes, there has been a considerable dispute as to whether a partnership is a legal entity or merely an aggregate of persons acting together.

There are two opposing theories on the nature of a partnership. One theory sometimes called the *entity theory,* is that a partnership is a distinct and separate entity from the partners, just as a corporation is a distinct and separate entity from the stockholders. The other, called the *aggregate theory,* is that partners are coowners of the firm and the firm property. Under the entity theory, a partner can deal with his firm just as if it were another entity. The aggregate theory views dealings between partner and partnership as a combination of a deal between one partner and his other partners and another deal with himself. Consequently, a particular transaction may result in different outcomes from a legal and tax viewpoint. The entity theory cannot be reconciled with the basic principle of partnership law that each partner is liable and responsible for partnership debts and obligations.

A review of the Uniform Act indicates that many of its rules are based on the entity theory. The Act provided for the ownership and conveyance of property in the firm's name, the continuity of the partnership notwithstanding the assignment of a partner's interest, the priority of partnership creditors in reference to partnership assets, and the fiduciary duty of a partner to the firm. The Act does apply the aggregate theory in establishing joint and several liablity for partners.

Statutes may, of course, specifically treat partnerships as entities. The Federal Bankruptcy Act treats a partnership as a distinct legal entity, as does the Uniform Commercial Code. One of the important points in the area of partnership taxation is that the partnership, as such, is not a taxable entity. It is merely a form of doing business by two or more persons who are liable for any tax in their individual capacities. Each partner picks up his or her share of the partnership's income or loss and reports them as part of his or her personal income or loss on his or her income tax returns.

The result is that the courts frequently hold that, in some respects and for some purposes, a partnership may be regarded as a legal entity. It is equally well settled that it is not such an entity as is a natural person or a corporation, and that its status as an independent entity is limited and incomplete. The courts point out that a partnership is an entity only for certain limited purposes, such as for facilitating transfers of property, marshalling assets, and protecting the business operations against the impact of personal involvement of the partners, or for other purposes.

Limited Partnership

Most states have special statutes which authorize the formation of limited partnerships. These permit individuals, upon compliance with the statutory requirements, to contribute specified sums to the capital of a partnership firm, and then limit their liability to the amount of their capital contribution. This is somewhat like the relationship of a stockholder to a corporation.

The general purpose of the Uniform Limited Partnership Act, which has been adopted in all states except Louisiana, Kentucky, and Wyoming, is to allow a form of business enterprise, other than a corporation, in which persons can invest their money without becoming liable as general partners for all debts of the partnership.

According to the Uniform Limited Partnership Act a limited partnership is formed by two or more persons under that Act, having as members one or more general partners and one or more limited partners. The Act specifically declares that limited partners, basically interested in investing, are not bound by the obligations of participating in the partnership. The general partner's rights, powers, and obligations are similar to those of partners in a general partnership.

The general partner may become individually liable for all the debts of the firm. He or she is accountable to other partners as a fiduciary. The Uniform Limited Partnership Act restricts his or her authority in a number of

16

ways. It also provides that he or she may be a general partner and a limited partner in the same partnership at the same time. In this situation this person has all the rights, powers, limitations, and liabilities of a general partner.

The Uniform Limited Partnership Act provides that a partnership may carry on any business which a partnership without limited partners may carry on, except those specified in the Act. Generally, a limited partnership may not engage in the banking or insurance businesses. In some states there are no such business limitations. Check your local statutes for specific business information.

Partnerships Compared with Other Entities
Corporations

A partnership is clearly distinguishable from a corporation. A corporation is an artificial person or entity created by law as the representative of those persons who contribute to, or become holders of, shares in the property entrusted to it for a common purpose. A corporation is a separate entity distinct from its individual members or stockholders, who, as natural persons, are merged in the corporate identity. The stockholders are generally not personally liable for any of the obligations of the corporation. On the other hand, each partner is individually liable for the debts and obligations of a partnership and for the acts of the other partners, so far as the acts are within the scope or apparent scope of their authority as partners. A corporation can act only through a direct vote of the shareholders or by officers or agents authorized for the purpose, and the shareholders of the corporation, as such, cannot bind the corporation. But in a partnership each member binds as a principal.

Although a corporation can, in effect, be owned by one shareholder, a single individual cannot be the owner of a partnership. The law does not permit a partnership to do business under the guise of a corporation. One of the essential elements of a partnership is joint ownership.

Sole Proprietorship

In a sole proprietorship the individual person is wholly and personally liable for all of his or her debts without regard to whether they may be incurred for personal or business reasons. He or she is a single, legal entity who cannot separate business debts or assets from those incurred personally. The sole proprietor is also in absolute and complete charge of the management and control of the business. There are tax shelters available to an individual that may not be available to other business organizations.

Joint Venture

A joint venture is an association of two or more persons to carry out a single business for profit which is usually, but not necessarily, limited to a single transaction. Liability is limited only by the fact that it is usually a single transaction and by the duration which is usually limited to a short period of time. The joint venture is governed by the same basic principles of law as are partnerships.

It is sometimes difficult to distinguish cases between joint ventures and partnerships. The legal relationships of the parties to a joint venture and the nature of their associations are quite similar and closely akin to a partnership. Despite the similarities, there are important distinctions between the two, the most important being the single nature of joint venture, the fact that loss-sharing is not essential, and the eligibility of corporations for membership.

A partnership is also to be distinguished from a *grubstake arrangement,* a very loose, informal compact whereby one party undertakes to supply finances and equipment which another party uses in discovering and locating mineral claims, after which the two parties share in any claims located as a result of such operations.

Joint and Common Ownership of Property

A partnership is different from all types of joint ownership of real and personal property. Although joint ownership of property is an essential element of a partnership, joint ownership, in and of itself, is not sufficient to constitute a legal partnership. Partnership property has many of the characteristics of an estate in common and of joint tenancy or cotenancy, however, the interest of

19

the partners in the firm property, under the Uniform Partnership Act, is called tenancy in partnership. A partnership arises out of a contract between the parties, whereas a joint ownership in property may be created by operation of law.

Non-Profit Associations

Since by definition a partnership must carry on a business for profit, it is generally recognized that a non-profit organization is different. Among these types of organizations not considered partnerships are fraternal orders, beneficial societies, patriotic organizations, civic societies, political committees or parties, religious organizations or societies, and sport or recreation associations.

Other associations which do not earn profits, although they may be formed for the purpose of achieving economic benefits for their members, would not qualify as legal partnerships. Included in this category are trade and professional associations and labor unions. However, the members of a voluntary association of individuals or of an unincorporated company organized for profit may be considered partners in their relationship to third persons.

Partnership Associations

A partnership association is a unique business organization which closely resembles the corporation. Members enjoy limited liability and the association is a separate entity for most purposes. The members have the right to control membership in the association. Interests in the association can be transferred, but the new owner may not participate in the management of the business unless he is elected to membership. These organizations are permitted in only a few states, and you should carefully check the particular statute before utilizing it. The main purpose is to enable persons desiring to combine their capital in any business enterprise to do so without incurring the general liability of partners, or the risk of having the business taken out of the control of those in whom it was placed without the original members' consent.

Joint Stock Company

A joint stock company is an association of individuals possessing a common capital divided into shares that represent the interests owned by the members. The shares are transferable without the consent of the other members and there is no dissolution upon the death, bankruptcy, or insanity of a member. It is like a corporation in that it has a separate name, but it is like a partnership in that there is unlimited liability of members.

Trust

A trust, in this sense, is an agreement (almost invariably in writing) in which one person or persons (called settlor or donor) conveys assets or property to another person or persons (called trustee) for the use and benefit of another person or persons (called beneficiary). The property is held, administered, and maintained in accordance with the instruction by the settlor contained in the written agreement.

A partnership is distinguishable from a trust in that a partnership involves joint ownership while a trust involves representative ownership. A trustee has a fiduciary duty to the beneficiary, just as a partner has to another partner, however, the converse is not true. A beneficiary has no duty or obligation to the trustee. Moreover, the beneficiary of a trust does not usually become involved in the management or operation of the trust as do partners. In a trust situation, the trustee is not ordinarily responsible for any losses or profits from the administration of the trust. Although partnerships and trusts have similarities, it is easy to specify in a written document just what arrangements the parties intend.

Selection of Your Business Organization

The factors typically discussed and considered in the process of selecting a business organization include (1) simplicity, (2) organizational flexibility, (3) financing, (4) continuity, (5) transferability of interests, (6) goodwill, (7) estate liquidity, (8) splitting of income among family members, (9) expenses involved in organization, (10) personal liability exposure, (11) centralization of management and control, and (12) tax factors.

You will need to make an analysis of your situation,

consider the relative importance and significance of the various factors involved, and make a selection which will comply with most of your needs. Generally, the exposure to personal liability is one of the negative factors in a partnership. There are many tax advantages in the partnership form of business organization even though the Tax Reform Act of 1976 placed some restrictions on the "at risk" requirements.

2

Preparation of Your Own
Partnership Agreement

A partnership, as a type of voluntary association, must find its basis in an expressed or implied agreement between the partners. The agreement, like most other contracts, need not be in writing to be legally binding. But you are strongly advised to insist upon a written agreement. There is always the problem of proving the existence of a partnership and, if there is no written agreement, this can be troublesome. Moreover, if the agreement was not in writing, when disputes arise as to its terms and conditions, usually after the parties have some disagreement, the question of what was intended in the beginning may never be resolved satisfactorily. If, after full discussions, a carefully drafted agreement is signed, there can be far less doubt about the intent and understanding of the parties.

Also, keep in mind that there are some situations in which an agreement must be in writing and signed by the parties to be legally valid. Those are the situations listed under your state statute of frauds. Usually included within this statute are real estate transactions, agreements that by their terms are not to be performed within one year after the making thereof, and agreements to answer for the debt, default, or miscarriage of another. A word to the wise—when in doubt, put it in writing.

There may be major tax factors that suggest having a written agreement. The Uniform Act provides that a partnership is subject to the extensive and detailed regulations of your state statutes unless you have a written agreement to the contrary. It is extremely important to you to create a written document that clearly reflects the rights and obligations that the parties intend to assume in their association with you. The topics listed in this book which you should consider in preparing a partnership agreement are taken from the typical transactions of the business community, and are selected with a view of avoiding disputes and disagreements. To the extent that you can avoid one single lawsuit, you will have saved your money, time, frustration, and embarrassment.

The Partnership Agreement

A contract, express or implied, is essential to the formation of a partnership. The words "contract" and "agreement," as used in this book, are synonymous. A contract is a promise, or set of promises, for the breach of which the law gives a remedy, or for the performance of which the law recognizes a duty. The duties and obligations of partners arising from a partnership agreement are regulated as far as they are covered by the written contract. A written agreement between partners constitutes the measure of the partner's rights and obligations. The written agreement may include practically any provision you desire so long as it is lawful. Where the written agreement does not cover situations or questions which arise, they are determined under applicable statutory law. If a question is not answered by the provisions of the statutes, it will be controlled by common law rules.

The existence of a partnership may be proven by transactions, conduct, and declarations in situations where there is no written agreement. As in the case of any contract, the consent of the parties is required to make a partnership contract enforceable. You cannot be made a partner by operation of law alone, but only by your voluntary acts. The Uniform Act provides that no person can become a member of a partnership without the consent of all the partners. A third person may charge another with partnership liability even in the absence of the existence of an actual partnership relation if there has been conduct leading the third person to believe there was a partnership. Such liability can be imposed on the alleged partner only upon the basis of his voluntary conduct indicating a partnership relation or upon the ground of his having permitted others to hold him out as partner. This is called partnership by estoppel. (See

Partners as to Third Persons—Estoppel.) This rule presents another strong reason for you to insist upon a written agreement to govern any business transaction in which you wish to participate.

Tests or Indicia of Partnerships

In determining whether a partnership exists, the courts will take numerous factors into account. Where parties expressly agree to unite their property and services as joint owners to carry on a business for a profit, and to share the profits and losses in stated proportions, there exists an agreement that clearly creates a partnership. But where the agreement between persons engaged in a business enterprise which is supposed to create a partnership relation is uncertain in its terms, as is often the case, or where the persons have never executed a formal, written expression of their relation, the courts have encountered great difficulty in formulating tests by which to determine the existence or nonexistence of a partnership relation. Reports are abundant with cases applying differing tests and indicia of a partnership relation, and differing conclusions have been reached, with the result that the decisions are so conflicting on the subject that it is impossible to reconcile them. These perplexing problems were among the many reasons that prompted the drafting of the Uniform Act, and the reasons for the advice to put your agreements in writing.

The Uniform Act provides certain rules for determining whether a partnership exists. But these rules are not all inclusive. Mainly, they are refinements of previous rules established by the courts. The draftsmen of the Act tacitly acknowledged the fact that a partnership is a contractual relationship that may vary in form and substance in an almost infinite variety of ways, by stating in the most general language an assortment of rules to be considered in determining whether a partnership exists.

In the last analysis, there is no arbitrary test for determining the existence of a partnership, and each case must be decided according to its particular facts. Confusion in the interpretation and application of decisions results when the tests are applied indiscriminately without keeping in mind a certain indication of partnership may be of considerable significance in one case and not in another. Generally, the elements considered critical to the existence of a partnership are intention of two or more persons to be partners, sharing of profits and losses, joint ownership and control of the capital assets or property of the group, and joint control and management of the business.

Sharing of Profits

Under the English doctrine from 1600 to 1850, which was followed by the American decisions (1776–1900), persons sharing the profits of a commercial enterprise were liable to creditors as if they were actual partners. These

29

early authorities treated the sharing of the profits as a conclusive test of the existence of a partnership, particularly as to third persons. Some courts also adopted this test in situations in which the rights of the parties, among themselves, were involved. The reason given for this test was that by taking part in the profits, there was taken from the creditors a part of that fund which was a security for the payment of their debts. In the course of time, important exceptions were introduced. Under these exceptions the early rule was not applied where the participant did not receive the profits as "principal or as profits," or where the profits were received as compensation for services rendered or in payment as rent to a landlord, or as a debt or interest on a loan. Ultimately the rule itself was abolished.

The current view, adopted by most courts, is that the sharing of profits is not, of itself, sufficiently conclusive to show the existence of a partnership relation. Participation in the profits does not necessarily make the recipient a legal partner, especially where there is no intention, joint ownership of the business, or other essentials of a valid partnership. In other words, participation in the profits is only regarded as a circumstance to be considered, among others, in determining whether or not a partnership existed. In order for a partnership to exist, there must be an ownership interest in the profits of the business.

Joint Ownership of Property

Although the profit and loss category is the most significant, it is not, in and of itself, sufficient to constitute a partnership. The ownership of the assets of a going business is also an important factor in determining whether a partnership exists. (See Chapter 4, Property Rights of Partners.)

Joint Management and Control of Business

Where one owns an interest in property and shares in the profits and losses, it is almost certain that he or she will exercise some degree of control over the management of the business. This is, again, only one of the factors that the courts examine in deciding on the existence of a partnership. Of course, the final determination is a question of fact and will depend upon the conclusions reached by a judge or jury based upon an evaluation of all of the facts and circumstances involved in a transaction. It is easy to see that a written agreement would eliminate the necessity of going through such a fact-finding procedure.

Factors Tending to Show One
Rendering Services a Partner

Various factors will determine whether a relationship is one of partnership or of employment. A person rendering services does not become a partner merely because he or she receives a share of the profits of the business, but an agreement to share losses as well as profits is a strong indication of the existence of a partnership. The fact that a party rendering services assumes financial obligations by agreeing to make capital contributions, or by furnishing credit, or by participating in the expenses necessary to produce profits, has been held suggestive of a partnership contract, and conversely, the lack of any obligations of this kind has been held to indicate an employment contract.

The fact that one rendering services for another is possessed, jointly with the other party or parties to the contract, of a property right in lands, chattels, moneys, or assets which are used to produce the profits, tends to indicate a partnership relation, and conversely, the lack of such property right suggests an employment contract. Where a party rendering services has rights of managing and determining the policies of the enterprise equal with those of the other party or parties to the contract, or permits the use of his or her name in the business operation, tends to indicate a partnership.

The Uniform Act defines a partnership and states the rules for determining the existence of a partnership as follows:

NATURE OF A PARTNERSHIP

Section 6. Partnership Defined

(1) A partnership is an association of two or more persons to carry on as coowners a business for profit.

(2) But an association formed under any other statute of this state, or any statute adopted by authority, other than the authority of this state, is not a partnership under

this act unless such association would have been a partnership in this state prior to the adoption of this act; but this act shall apply to limited partnerships except in so far as the statutes relating to such partnerships are inconsistent herewith.

Section 7. Rules for Determining the Existence of a Partnership

In determining whether a partnership exists, these rules shall apply:

(1) Except as provided by section 16, persons who are not partners as to each other are not partners as to third persons.

(2) Joint tenancy, tenancy in common, tenancy by the entireties, joint property, common property, or part ownership does not of itself establish a partnership, whether such coowners do or do not share any profits made by the use of the property.

(3) The sharing of gross returns does not of itself establish a partnership, whether or not the persons sharing them have a joint or common right or interest in any property from which the returns are derived.

(4) The receipt by a person of a share of the profits of a business is prima facie evidence that he is a partner in the business, but no such inference shall be drawn if such profits were received in payment:

(a) As a debt by installments or otherwise,

(b) As wages of an employee or rent to a landlord,

(c) As an annuity to a widow or representative of a deceased partner,

(d) As interest on a loan, though the amount of payment vary with the profits of the business,

(e) As the consideration for the sale of a goodwill of a business or other property by installments or otherwise.

Section 8. Partnership Property

(1) All property originally brought into the partnership stock or subsequently acquired by purchase or otherwise, on account of the partnership, is partnership property.

(2) Unless the contrary intention appears, property acquired with partnership funds is partnership property.

(3) Any estate in real property may be acquired in the partnership name. Title so acquired can be conveyed only in the partnership name.

(4) A conveyance to a partnership in the partnership name, though without words of inheritance, passes the entire estate of the grantor unless a contrary intent appears.

Partners as to Third Persons—Estoppel

At common law, that is, prior to the adoption of the Uniform Act, the courts had frequently stated that persons who were not partners as to each other, but who held themselves out as partners, were partners as to third persons, and were subject to the liabilities of partners. Some cases which were decided after the adoption of the Uniform Act still base the liability of individuals on the fact that they are partners as to third persons. This liability is based on the doctrine of estoppel, and on the policy of the law seeking to prevent frauds on those who lend their money on the apparent credit of those who are held out as partners. But in view of the specific provisions of the Uniform Act, the courts generally recognize that persons who are not partners, as among themselves, are not partners as to third persons, unless the principle of estoppel is applicable. The modern rule is that, while technically there is no such status as partners as to third persons, in some instances persons may, under the application of the doctrine of estoppel, become liable as if they were partners.

The liability as a partner of a person who holds himself or herself out as a partner, or permits others to do so, is predicated on the doctrine of equitable estoppel. This is the common law rule which is codified in the Uniform Code. While the existence of a partnership may be proved by any competent evidence, the best evidence consists of the agreement or contract between the parties.

The provision in the Uniform Act relating to partnership by estoppel is as follows:

Section 16. Partnership by Estoppel

(1) When a person, by words spoken or written or by conduct, represents himself, or consents to another representing him to any one, as a partner in an existing partnership or with one or more persons not actually partners, he is liable to any such person to whom such representation has been made, who has, on the faith of such representation, given credit to the actual or apparent partnership, and if he has made such representation or consented to its being made in a public manner he is liable to such person, whether the representation has or has not been made or communicated to such person so giving credit by or with the knowledge of the apparent partner making the representation or consenting to its being made.

(a) When a partnership liability results, he is liable as

though he were an actual member of the partnership.

(b) When no partnership liability results, he is liable jointly with the other persons, if any, so consenting to the contract or representation as to incur liability, otherwise separately.

(2) When a person has been thus represented to be a partner in an existing partnership, or with one or more persons not actual partners, he is an agent of the persons consenting to such representation to bind them to the same extent and in the same manner as though he were a partner in fact, with respect to persons who rely upon the representation. Where all the members of the existing partnership consent to the representation, a partnership act or obligation results; but in all other cases it is the joint act or obligation of the person acting and the persons consenting to the representation.

Preparing Your Contract

You can benefit from all of the past disputes and mistakes which have occurred between partners if you study the rules and understand and appreciate the problems which may arise provided, of course, you prepare a written agreement for your business transactions before they get under way—before it is too late.

In order to give you a full and complete understanding of the requirements for a written partnership agreement, each and every part of a full, complete, comprehensive, and legally valid partnership agreement is listed and discussed below. Alternative, additional, and supplemental provisions and suggestions are also provided. In addition, several sample partnership agreements will be given. You will be able to select one of the simple agreements, or parts of several of them, and by adding, deleting, and amending as appropriate, draft your own partnership agreement which has all of the items necessary for a final, formal business document. However, it is strongly recommended that you do not attempt to prepare your partnership agreement until you have carefully read and studied the entire text of this book.

Checklist of Facts and Information You Should Consider in Preparing Your Partnership Agreement

Before you start any work on your partnership agreement, you should carefully study the checklist which follows, and make provisions for all items which may arise in connection with your business arrangements. By doing this you will be certain to avoid or resolve disputes, disagreements, and misunderstandings that typically arise in the conduct of business.

1. In what name will the partnership business be conducted?
2. What are the names and addresses of the partners?
3. What type of business is to be conducted?
4. Where is the business to be located?
5. Term of existence:
   (a) What date is the business to be started?
   (b) How long is the business to continue?

6. Capital of the partnership:

    (a) How much capital is to be invested by each partner?

    (b) How much is to be invested in cash?

    (c) How much is to be invested in property other than cash?

    (d) When is property or cash to be paid into partnership?

    (e) What arrangements are to be made for additional capital?

7. How are profits and losses to be divided between the partners?

8. What salaries are partners to receive?

9. Are partners to be permitted drawing accounts?

10. Are partners to receive interest on capital investment?

11. Duties of partners:

    (a) Are partners to devote their time exclusively to the business?

    (b) What specific functions will each partner perform?

    (c) What are the rights of each partner in management of the partnership business?

12. Disposal of partnership interest:

    (a) Will partner be permitted to sell his or her interest?

    (b) Should partner be prohibited from selling his or her interest?

13. Banking of funds:

    (a) What is the name of bank?

(b) Who is to sign checks?

14. Books of account:

    (a) Where are the books to be kept?

    (b) What provisions are to be made for auditing by accountants?

15. Termination or dissolution:

    (a) How shall the partnership be terminated?

    (b) Does either partner have the right to continue business upon termination?

    (c) What are the rights of partners to return of capital contributions?

    (d) What procedure shall be used to liquidate the business?

16. Death of partners:

    (a) What are the rights of the survivors?

    (b) What is the purchase price of decedents' interest or how shall it be determined?

    (c) What provision is to be made to continue the business?

    (d) What provision is to be made to liquidate the business?

17. Disability of partners:

    (a) What are the rights of a partner who has been disabled or is unable to perform his or her duties as partner upon disability?

    (b) What are the rights of partners to purchase a disabled partner's share in the partnership?

18. Are provisions to be made for admitting additional partners?
19. Are provisions to be made for arbitration of controversies?
20. Are provisions to be made for retirement of partners?
21. Are provisions to be made to expel a partner whose misconduct, inattention to business, or other action seriously injures the business?
22. Use of partnership name:
    (a) May partnership name be continued upon the death of partner?
    (b) May partnership name be continued upon the retirement of partner?
    (c) May partnership name be continued upon sale of business?
23. How is title to partnership assets to be taken?
24. Shall provision be made not to divulge trade secrets?
25. Shall provision be made for retiring partners not to compete in business?
26. Shall provision be made that no partner shall become maker, endorser, or surety of any obligation without consent?
27. What restrictions shall be made on outside activities of partners?
28. Are partners to be bonded?
29. Are provisions to be made for goodwill of business?
30. Are provisions to be made for life insurance?

31. Are partners to be limited in any manner as to their power or authority to act as agent of the partnership?
32. Are provisions to be made to amend this partnership agreement?

When you have determined the answers to these questions, you will be able to select the appropriate parts for your partnership agreement from the forms listed in this book. You will begin your agreement with introductory clauses.

SAMPLE PARTNERSHIP AGREEMENT FORMS

Introductory Clauses

Most written agreements begin with the date, identification of the parties, statement of the place of residence of each, and a statement of the purpose and intention of the written document. Although these are not absolutely essential to the validity of a contract, they are important, helpful, and should appear at some place in the document. There are many different forms that are frequently used, and the following are the most popular samples. Begin your agreement with one of these statements.

Sample 1:

This agreement of partnership made and entered into this ____ day of _____ , 19__ , by and between _____ , _____ , and _____ , all of the City of _____ , County of _____ , State of _____ , witness and agree as follows:

41

Sample 2:

It is hereby understood and agreed between _____ , party of the first part, and _____ , party of the second part, that _____ .

Sample 3:

This Partnership Agreement entered into on _____ , between _____ , of _____ , and _____ _____ , of _____ , Witnesseth:

Name of Partnership or Business

Sample 1:

The firm name of the said partnership shall be _____ _____ .

Sample 2:

The business of the said partnership shall be carried on under the firm name of _____ .

Duration

Term

Sample 1:

This partnership shall continue for the term of _____ years from the date of this agreement.

Sample 2:

This partnership shall continue until the death of the parties, unless previously terminated, but either party may terminate it at will upon giving _____ days' notice to the other partners.

Sample 3:

The said _____ , _____ , _____ ____ , and _____ , and the survivors of them, will become and remain partners in the business of _____ from the ____ day of _____ , 19____ , during the term of _____ years, if they or any two of them shall so long live, under the firm name of _____ ____ , subject, nevertheless, to termination as hereinafter provided.

After Retirement or Death of Partner

Sample 1:

Any partner may retire from the partnership on or at any time after the _____ day of _____ , 19____ , on giving not less than ____ months' previous written notice to the others of his intention to do so, and at the expiration of such notice, the partnership shall terminate so far as regards the partner giving or leaving such notice, but not as between the remaining partners.

Sample 2:

The death of any partner shall not dissolve the partnership between the remaining partners.

Sample 3:

Should any partner die during the term of this agreement, the firm shall not be dissolved thereupon, but the business shall be continued by the survivors until the expiration of the term, the estate of the deceased partner to bear the same share in profits and losses as would have been received and borne by the deceased partner, had he lived.

Place of Business

Sample 1:

The partnership business and operations shall be carried on at _____ _____ , or at such other places as the partners shall from time to time determine.

Sample 2:

The offices of said firm shall be situated at _____ _____

Purpose

Sample 1:

This partnership shall be for the purpose of buying, selling, and dealing in _____ .

Sample 2:

The object of this partnership shall be to engage generally in the business of _____ , and its allied arts and trades, and of buying, selling, and generally dealing in all goods, merchandise, and supplies incidental thereto.

Sample 3:

This partnership is for the purpose of buying, developing, and selling a certain tract of land described as follows: _____

_____ ,

and for no other purpose.

Capital

General Forms

Sample 1:

The capital of the partnership shall be _____ dollars, and each partner shall contribute equally thereto (or in the shares or proportions following, namely _____) or in such shares as may from time to time be agreed upon in writing.

Sample 2:

Each partner shall leave in the business each year as an addition to the partnership capital an amount equal to _____ of the profits distributable to him at the time of each annual accounting.

Sample 3:

The stock in trade and plant now owned by the said _____ shall be taken to be of the value of _____ dollars, and shall become the partnership property of such valuation, and shall be credited to the said _____ on account of the capital which he is to contribute.

One Partner Furnishing Capital

The said _____ shall at once bring into the business the sum of _____ dollars as capital, which shall be employed in the said business, and for the benefit of the partnership, during the partnership term, without any allowance of interest for its use, and shall, from time to time, at the request of the said _____ , advance and bring into the said business such further sums of money (not exceeding the sum of _____ dollars in any one year, nor exceeding, together with the said sum of _____ dollars, the total sum of _____ dollars) as shall, in the opinion of the said _____ _____ , be required for carrying on the said business, and shall be allowed interest on such further advances at the rate of ____ percent per annum out of the profits of the said business, before any division of such profits.

One Partner Without Capital

The said _____ shall furnish the sum of _____ dollars as capital to carry on the business. The said _____ shall devote his entire time, services, and skill to the management of the business and shall not be required to contribute to the capital stock of the partnership, and shall share equally in profits and losses (including depreciation in capital) with the other partners.

Increase of Capital

If, at any time hereafter, further capital shall be required for carrying on the business, and a majority of the partners shall determine to increase the capital, the additional capital shall be advanced by the partners in equal shares (or in such proportions as they have respectively contributed to the original capital of the firm).

Additional Capital

If any partner shall, with the other partners' consent, bring in additional capital, or leave any part of his profits in the business, the same shall be considered a debt due to him from the partnership, and shall bear interest at the rate of ____ percent per annum, and shall not be drawn out except upon giving ____ calendar months' written notice; and the partner who has brought in additional capital or left in part of his profits shall be bound to draw out the same on a like notice given to him by the other partners, and at the expiration of such notice interest shall cease to be payable thereon.

Dormant Partner

Said _____ shall contribute the sum of _____ dollars to the firm, as his share of the capital thereof, but shall have no active part in the management of the business of the firm, nor shall his name be used in the firm name, nor in any advertising of the firm, but shall be entitled to ____ percent of the profits, if any, of the firm, and shall bear ____ percent of the losses, if any, of the firm.

Advances

Any partner may from time to time, with the consent of the others, advance any sums of money to the firm by way of loan, and every such advance shall bear interest at the rate of ____ percent per annum, from the time of making the advance until repayment thereof, and may be withdrawn at any time on ____ months' notice.

Expenses

All rent, expenses for repairs or improvements, all taxes, premiums of insurance, salaries and wages, and any and all other reasonable and necessary expenses, losses and damages which may be incurred in carrying on the partnership business (and the interest on the capital, payable to the respective partners), shall be paid out of the receipts and earnings of the said business, and in case such receipts and earnings are insufficient to pay such charges, the said partners shall contribute thereto in the shares or proportions in which they are entitled to the profits of the business.

Profits, Compensation, and Drawing Accounts

Division of Profits and Losses

Sample 1:

Each partner herein shall share in all profits or losses of the business in the same proportion as his share in the capital of the firm bears to the total capital of the firm.

Sample 2:

The profits and losses shall belong to, and be borne by, _____ ____ and _____ in equal shares.

Guaranty of Profits

In case the share of _____ in the net profits shall in any year be less than _____ dollars, such share shall in every such year be made up to _____ dollars by the other partners, by contributions in proportion to the shares in which they are entitled to the net profits.

Drawing Accounts

Each partner shall be at liberty, from time to time, to draw out of the business any sum or sums of money, not exceeding the sum of _____ dollars per month, for his own use; all such sums, at the time of drawing the same, to be entered in the cashbook, and to be duly accounted for on every settlement of accounts and divisions of the profits of the business.

Salary

_____ , the managing partner, shall receive as compensation during the term of this agreement a salary of $ _____ per month in addition to his share of the profits, and the salary shall be considered as an expense of the firm.

Regular Meetings

On Friday of each week, at 9:00 a.m., there shall be a meeting of the partners, at the office of the firm, for the purpose of going over expense accounts for the preceding week, and for the further purpose of discussing and acting upon the general conduct of the business of the partnership. For any matters within the scope of the business, and within this or supplemental contracts, a majority of the partners present at any such meeting shall prevail. Any change of the scope or nature of the business, however, shall not be made except by and with the knowledge and consent of all of the partners.

Books and Accounts

Keeping Accounts

Proper books of accounts shall be kept at the office of the firm, in which shall be entered all the dealings and transactions of the partnership. The books shall at all times be open to the inspection of all or any of the partners, and be kept constantly posted and current.

Taking Accounts

The partners, once in each year, namely, on the ____ day of _____ in each and every year, or more often if necessary, shall make and render, each to the other, full and correct inventories and accounts of all profits and increase by them or either of them made, and of all losses by them or either of them sustained; and also of all payments, receipts, disbursements, and all other things by them made, received, disbursed, acted, done, or suffered in the partnership and business; and upon the rendering of every such account shall clear, adjust, pay, and deliver, each to the other, their just share of the profits so made as aforesaid.

Restrictions on Authority of Partners

Limits upon Contracts by One Partner

Neither partner, without the previous consent in writing of the others, shall buy or sell or enter into any contract for the purchase or sale of any goods or other articles amounting to the value of _____ dollars or more.

Negotiable Paper

All checks, notes, and other writings pledging the credit or affecting the property of the partnership, shall be signed by _____ or _____ , and not otherwise.

Bonds and Securities

Whenever there shall be occasion to give any bond, note, bill, or other security for the payment of any money on account of the partnership, the same shall be respectively signed and executed by all the partners.

Suretyship

No partner shall, without the others' previous written consent, enter into any bond, or become bail, surety, or security, for any person.

Extending Credit

No partner shall lend any money, or give credit to, or have dealings on behalf of the partnership with, any person, partnership, or corporation whom the other partners or partner shall have forbidden him to trust or deal with; and if he shall act contrary to this provision, he shall repay to the partnership any loss which may have been incurred thereby.

Pledging Credit

No partner shall pledge the credit of the firm or use any money, goods, or effects of the partnership except in the ordinary course of business, and upon the account or for the benefit of the partnership.

Release of Debts

No partner shall, without consent of the others, compound, release, or discharge any debt which shall be due or owing to the partnership, without receiving the full amount thereof.

Hiring Employees

No partner shall hire or dismiss, unless in case of gross misconduct, any clerk or any other person in the employment of the partnership, without the other partners' consent.

Retirement of Partner

Withdrawal of Partner

Any partner may retire at any time from the partnership, upon giving written notice of his intention to do so, to the other partners personally, and the partnership shall determine as to him ____ months after the date of said notice; but the other partners may purchase his interest at a fair valuation and carry on the business.

Retiring Partner Not to Compete

In the event of any of the said partners retiring as aforesaid, he shall not, during the remainder of the term of the said partnership, carry on or engage or be interested, directly or indirectly, in any other business competing or interfering with the business of the firm, subject, however, to any applicable statute to the contrary.

Retiring Partner to Be Indemnified

In case any partner shall at any time withdraw from the partnership, and shall sell his interest therein to the remaining partners, or, in case of dissolution, when a part of said partners shall purchase the interest of the other partners, then such purchasing partners shall give good and sufficient bond to such withdrawing partner, to the reasonable satisfaction of such withdrawing partner, in an amount equal to the amount of the debts of the firm, conditioned on the payment in full of all outstanding debts of said firm, when due, and for the savings of such withdrawing partner, of any loss which might occur to such withdrawing partner, by reason of the nonpayment of such debts as herein provided.

Dissolution

Dissolution in Case of Loss

In case the net assets of the partnership shall at any time fall below the sum of _____ dollars, then any member thereof, in spite of the fact that the partnership has not expired by lapse of time, may withdraw from the firm, and commence an action for the dissolution of the firm.

50

Winding up Business

Upon dissolution of the partnership, a full and general account of the firm assets, liabilities, and transactions shall be taken, and the assets and property of the firm shall, as soon as practicable, be sold, the debts due the partnership collected, the proceeds to be applied, first, in the discharge of the firm liabilities and the expenses of liquidating the same; and next, in payment to each partner or his representatives of any unpaid interest or profits belonging to him, and of his share of the capital; and the surplus, if any, shall be divided between the partners or their representatives in the shares in which they contributed the firm capital; and the partners or their representatives shall execute all requisite or proper instruments for facilitating the collection and division of the partnership property and for their mutual indemnity and release.

Goodwill

On the death or retirement of any partner no allowance (or an allowance) shall be made to him or his representatives in respect of the value of the goodwill of the said business.

Division of Property

At the expiration of this agreement the parties herein shall each give all possible aid to arrive at a just and true account of all the assets and liabilities. The assets, including the goodwill of said business, shall first be offered for sale to the partners herein, and the partner offering the most for the same shall be allowed to purchase the same. In case there is no partner who desires to purchase the assets, then the assets shall be sold to whomever shall pay the most therefor. In either event, all liabilities shall be paid for out of the proceeds of such sale. The net amount secured by such sale shall be divided among the parties, in proportion to their interest in the firm, at such time of dissolution.

Deceased Partner's Interest

The executors or administrators of any partner who shall die during the partnership, or any person or persons to whom he may, by will, bequeath his share in the partnership, shall be entitled to his share in the firm, capital stock, property, and effects, and may either continue as partner or partners in the business in respect and to the extent of his share and interest of such deceased partner, or may sell the same in the manner hereinabove provided with respect to a sale by any living partner of his share and interest.

Close of Contract

In witness whereof, we hereunto set our hands, this _____ day of _____ _____ , 19__ , at _____ , _____ .

_____   _____
(Witnesses, if any)   (Signatures)

Sample Partnership Agreements

The forms that follow contain the essentials for a clear, understandable agreement that you can easily add to or delete from to prepare a written agreement which expresses the understanding and intent of your situation.

You will note that the forms below include several complete partnership agreements and several alternative, additional, or supplemental provisions. In most situations, one of the form agreements, with minor changes, deletions, or additions, will suffice for completion of a proper agreement. In other situations, depending upon the particular facts and circumstances, and depending upon the answers to the check list questions, you can formulate a proper agreement by use of the appropriate provision in the list of forms. In the event you need to cover some special or unusual subject, simply add other paragraphs to spell out clearly the intent and agreement of the parties.

You should not have any of the provisions in the agreement which are, or may be construed as, contradictory, inconsistent, or confusing. Each provision should be discussed in detail by all partners before the agreement is executed. Having done this, you will have accomplished nearly everything any reasonable person could do to assure a smooth, successful, and rewarding business career.

FORM 1: General Partnership Agreement—Two Partners

This agreement made this ____ day of _____ , 19 __ , between _____ and _____ , both of the City of _____ , County of _____ , State of _____ _____ , witness and agree as follows:

1. The parties do hereby agree to form a partnership under the name of _____ for the purpose of conducting a _____ business.

2. The place at which the partnership is to conduct its business is _____ .

3. The partnership shall continue until dissolved by mutual agreement.

4. The capital of the partnership shall be contributed equally in cash by the partners.

5. The net profits of the partnership shall be divided equally between the partners, and the net losses shall be borne equally by them.

6. Neither partner shall receive any salary for services rendered to the partnership.

7. Each of the partners shall be permitted such drawing accounts as may be agreed upon between them.

8. Both partners are to devote their entire time and attention to the business. The partners shall have equal rights in the management of the partnership business.

9. The partnership books shall be kept at the place of business and shall be at all times open to inspection by either partner.

10. All funds of the partnership shall be deposited in its name in _____ _____ Bank, and all withdrawals therefrom are to be made upon checks signed by either partner.

11. Either partner may retire from the partnership at the expiration of any fiscal year by giving to the other partner _____ days' notice of his intention to do so. The remaining partner shall have the right either to purchase the retiring partner's interest or to terminate the partnership and liquidate the business. In the event the remaining partner elects to purchase the remaining interest of the retiring partner, the purchase price shall be equal to the book value of the retiring partner's interest in the partnership business as reflected in the partnership books. The purchase

price shall be paid by an initial cash payment of $ _____ , and the balance in ____ installments over a period of ____ years, and shall bear interest on the unpaid balance at the rate of ____ percent per annum.

12. Upon the death of either partner the surviving partner shall have the right either to purchase the interest of the decedent in the partnership or to terminate and liquidate the partnership business. If the surviving partner elects to purchase the decedent's interest, the terms and conditions shall be the same as set forth in the preceding paragraph. If the surviving partner does not elect to purchase the interest of the decedent in the partnership, he shall proceed with reasonable promptness to liquidate the business of the partnership.

IN WITNESS WHEREOF, the parties have signed this Agreement.

_____   _____

(Witnesses, if any)   (Signatures)

_____   _____

FORM 2: Partnership Agreement—Several Partners— Equal Contributions

This Agreement made this ____ day of _____ , 19 __ , between _____ , _____ , _____ , and _____ , all of the City of _____ , County of _____ , State of _____ , witness and agree as follows:

1. Name: The firm name of the partnership shall be _____ .
2. Purpose: The purpose of the partnership shall be _____ .
3. Office: The offices of the firm shall be located at _____ .
4. Commencement: The partnership shall commence _____ .
5. Duration: The partnership shall continue until it is dissolved or liquidated.
6. Capital: The capital of the partnership shall be contributed in equal amounts by each partner.
7. Capital Account: An individual capital account shall be maintained for each partner.
8. Withdrawal: No partner shall withdraw any of his capital without the consent of all partners.
9. Capital Gains and Losses: Capital gains and losses shall be shared equally among the partners.
10. Loans by Partners: Interest at the rate of ____ percent per annum shall be allowed on all loans made to the partnership and on all funds left with the firm which the partner would otherwise be entitled to withdraw.
11. Time Devoted to Business: Each partner shall devote his entire time, attention, and ability to the affairs of the partnership.
12. Vacations: Each partner shall be entitled to such vacations with salary as may be agreed on.
13. Sickness: When a partner is unable to devote his full time to partnership affairs for reasons of health or otherwise, he shall be entitled to receive such monthly salary and such share of profits as the partners shall determine by vote of the majority in interest.
14. Management: Each partner shall have equal voice in the conduct of the affairs of the business and all decisions shall be by vote of the majority. _____ shall act as General Manager to administer the

general affairs of the partnership and to carry out and put into effect the general policies and specific instructions of the majority of the partners.

15. Bank Accounts: The partnership shall maintain checking or other accounts in such bank or banks as the partners shall agree upon. Withdrawal shall be on the signature of _____ and co-signed by _____ .

16. Records: All books, records, and accounts of the partnership shall be maintained at the office of the partnership and shall be open to inspection at all times by all partners. For the purpose of partnership accounting and for income tax reporting, the partnership fiscal year shall end on the ____ day of _____ each year. At the end of each month, the books shall be balanced and an operating statement prepared and made available to each partner posting the results of operations during the previous month. The books shall be audited at the end of each fiscal year and statements prepared and supplied to all partners showing the results of operations.

17. Profits and Losses: The partners shall share equally in the profits and losses. As soon as practical after the accounting statements for each fiscal year are approved by all partners, the profits, after salaries of partners, shall be paid to the partners, provided there are funds available in excess of the working capital requirements.

18. Salaries: Until further agreed upon, each partner shall be entitled to a salary of _____ dollars, payable at the end of each month, provided payment of partners' salaries does not impair the capital of the partnership.

19. Limitations on Partners: No partner, without the consent of all other partners, shall borrow money on the partnership name for partnership purposes or utilize collateral owned by the partnership as security for such loans; assign, transfer, pledge, compromise, or release any of the claims or debts due to the partnership except on payment in full; consent to the arbitration of any dispute or controversy of the partnership; transfer firm assets; make, execute, or deliver any assignment for the benefit of creditors; make, execute, or deliver any bond, confession of judgment, guaranty bond, indemnity bond, or surety bond, or any contract to sell, bill of sale, deed, mortgage, lease relating to any substantial part of the partnership assets or his interest therein, make any purchases in excess of _____ dollars; or engage in any business or occupation without the consent of all other partners.

20. Retirement: Any partner shall have the right to retire from the partnership at the end of any accounting year.

(a) Written notice of intention to retire shall be served upon the other partners at the office of the partnership at least _____ days before the end of the accounting year.

(b) The retirement of any partner shall have no effect upon the continuation of the partnership business.

(c) The remaining partners shall have the right to either purchase the retiring partner's interest or to terminate and liquidate the business.

(d) If the remaining partners elect to purchase the interest of the retiring partner, they shall serve notice in writing of such an election upon the retiring partner at the office of the partnership within _____ days after receipt of his notice of intention to retire.

(e) The purchase price shall be _____ dollars payable in cash and the balance in _____ installments over a period of _____ years and shall be based on the partner's capital interest as set forth in the annual audit.

(f) No allowance shall be made for goodwill, trade name, patents, or other intangible assets, except as those assets have been reflected on the partnership books prior to the annual audit.

(g) If the remaining partners do not elect to purchase the interest of the retiring partner, the remaining partners shall proceed with reasonable promptness to liquidate the business of the partnership.

21. Death: Upon the death of any partner, the surviving partners shall have the right either to purchase the interest of the decedent in the partnership or to terminate and liquidate the partnership business.

(a) If the surviving partners elect to purchase the decedent's interest, they shall serve notice in writing of such election within _____ days after the death of the decedent, upon the executor or administrator of the decedent, or if at the time of such election, no legal representative has been appointed, upon any one of the known legal heirs at the last known address of such heir.

(b) The purchase price and payment thereof shall be the same as set forth in the previous paragraph, except that a physical inventory shall be taken and the partnership books shall be closed and an audit made at the close of business at the end of the current month.

(c) The continuing partners shall have the right to use the firm name of the partnership.

(d) Each of the partners shall have the right to purchase a portion of the decedent's partnership interest in the same proportion which his interest bears to the surviving partner's interest in the partnership.

(e) If the surviving partners do not elect to purchase the entire interest of the decedent, they shall proceed with reasonable promptness to liquidate the business.

(f) The surviving partners and the estates of the deceased partner shall share in the profits and losses of the business during the period of liquidation in the same proportions in which they shared such profits and losses prior to the death of the deceased partner, except that the decedent shall not be liable for losses in excess of the decedent's interest in the partnership at the time of his death.

(g) So long as any surviving partner shall devote his full time to the liquidation of the partnership business, he shall receive a salary at the same rate as he received immediately prior to the decedent's death.

(h) After the payment of partnership debts, the proceeds of liquidation shall be distributed as realized, first in discharge of the undrawn earnings of the partners, including the undrawn earnings of the decedent prior to his death, and the undrawn earnings of his estate during liquidation, then in such manner as to make the capital accounts of the partners proportionate to the capital accounts of the partnership as of the date of its organization, and then proportionately in discharge of the respective capital accounts.

IN WITNESS WHEREOF, the parties have signed and sealed this Agreement this _____ day of _____ , 19___ .

_____   _____
(Witnesses, if any)   (Signatures)

_____   _____

FORM 3: Partnership Agreement—Several Partners— Unequal Contributions

This Agreement made this ____ day of _____ , 19__ , between _____ , _____ , _____ , and _____ , all of the City of _____ , County of _____ , State of _____ , witness and agree as follows:

1. The parties do hereby form a partnership under the name of _____ _____ , to conduct a business of _____ .

2. The principal offices of the partnership shall be located at _____ _____ , in the City of _____ , State of _____ , and at such other place or places as may hereafter be agreed upon by the partners.

3. The partnership shall begin business on the ____ day of _____ , 19__ , and shall continue for ____ years from said date, or, unless sooner terminated, as herein provided, may be extended for another period or periods by the unanimous consent of the partners above named, evidenced by an endorsement upon this Agreement or by a separate instrument.

4. The capital of the partnership shall consist of _____ dollars of which _____ dollars shall be contributed by _____ , above named; _____ dollars by _____ , above named; _____ dollars by _____ , above named; and _____ dollars by _____ , above named.

5. The net profits and net losses of the partnership shall be divided by the partners in proportion to their capital investment.

6. No salaries as such shall be paid to the partners, but each shall be entitled to a drawing account of $ _____ per week, provided said drawing does not impair the capital investment of the partners, and so long as there remain sufficient sums to pay the debts of the partnership.

7. Each partner shall have an equal right in the management of the partnership business and each partner shall devote his entire time to the conduct of said business.

8. All funds of the partnership shall be deposited in its name in the _____ Bank or such other banks as may hereafter be

agreed upon between the partners, in such account or accounts as shall be designated by them, and all withdrawals therefrom are to be made by check, signed by any two partners.

9. The partnership shall maintain proper books of accounts of all transactions of the partnership at its place of business, and such books shall be open to inspection at all times to the partners.

10. No partner shall, without the consent of the other partners, compromise or release any debts due the said partnership except upon full payment thereof, or engage in any transaction on behalf of the said partnership of any kind other than those necessary for the transaction of the business of the said partnership, nor make any contract or account of the partnership requiring the expenditure of more than _____ dollars.

11. No partner shall, without the consent of all the other partners, make or endorse, either in the name of the said partnership or individually, any note, or act as an accommodation party, or otherwise become surety for any person. No partner shall, without the consent of all other partners, on behalf of the partnership, borrow or lend money to make, deliver, or accept any commercial paper or execute any mortgage, bond, lease, or other obligation requiring the payment of money, or purchase or contract to purchase or sell any property for or of the partnership other than the type of property bought and sold in the regular course of its business.

12. No partner shall, without the consent of all the other partners, assign, mortgage, or sell his share in the partnership or in its capital, assets, or property thereof, or enter into any agreement as a result of which any person shall become interested with him in the partnership, or do any act detrimental to the business interests of the partnership or which would make it impossible to carry on the ordinary business of the partnership.

13. Each partner shall have the right to retire from the partnership at the end of any fiscal year. Written notice of intention so to retire shall be served by the partner retiring upon the other partners at the place of business of the partnership at least ____ days before the end of such fiscal year. In case of the retirement of any partner, the remaining partners shall have the right to continue the partnership business or to terminate and liquidate it. If the remaining partners elect to purchase the interest of the retiring partner, they shall serve written notice of such election upon the retiring partner at the office of the partnership within ____ days after receipt of notice of his intention to retire.

14. In the event the remaining partners elect to purchase the interest of the retiring partner in the partnership, the price shall be equal to the book value of the retiring partner's share of the assets of the said partnership. In such event, the firm name shall thereafter be changed so as to remove therefrom the name of the retiring partner. The purchase price shall be paid without interest as follows: ____ percent in cash and the balance by the remaining partners making and delivering to the retiring partner a promissory note which shall be payable in monthly installments over a period of ____ years, bearing no interest. The retiring partner upon receiving the initial cash payment and the said promissory note shall execute and deliver to the remaining partners any and all instruments necessary and proper to transfer and convey to the remaining partners all partnership assets held in his name and his proportionate interest in the partnership assets.

15. If the remaining partners do not purchase the interest of the retiring partner in the partnership, the partners shall proceed with reasonable diligence and prudence to liquidate the business of the partnership. In such liquidation, the partnership assets, including the partnership name and goodwill of the said business, trade names, patents, and other intangible assets, shall be sold for such price as may reasonably be obtained for the same. The partners shall share equally in the profits and losses of the business during the period of liquidation and the proceeds realized from such liquidation shall be divided proportionately between the partners according to their capital investment.

16. Upon the death of any partner during the continuance of the partnership, the surviving partners shall have the right either to purchase the interest of the decedent in the partnership, or to terminate and liquidate the partnership business. If the surviving partners elect to purchase the decedent's interest, they shall serve notice in writing of such election upon the executor, administrator, or other legal representative of the said decedent, personally, within ____ days after the appointment of such legal representative, or if no such legal representative be appointed within ____ days after the death of the said deceased, then upon any one of the known heirs at law, next of kin, or distributees of the decedent at the last known address of such person, within ____ days after the termination of such days' period. If the surviving partners elect to purchase the interest of the

62

deceased partner in the said partnership, the purchase price, the method of payment, and the assets to be transferred shall be the same as previously stated herein with reference to the purchase of the interest of a retiring partner, except that in such event, the surviving partners shall be entitled to continue the use of the firm name of the partnership. All payments for the interest of said decedent in the said partnership shall be made to his duly appointed legal representative when he has been appointed and qualified. In the event that none has been appointed, the surviving partners shall at the time of service of notice hereinabove mentioned upon an heir at law, next of kin, or distributee of the decedent, at the same time serve upon him a demand that he cause such legal representative to be appointed. If such legal representative is not appointed at the time the surviving partners are to make such payment, it shall be extended until such legal representative has been appointed, and the surviving partners shall be entitled to hold the assets of the said partnership and use them in the conduct of the business thereof and shall be entitled to all profits received from the said business subsequent to the date of serving such notice.

17. If the surviving partners do not elect to purchase the interest of the decedent in the partnership, they shall proceed with reasonable diligence to liquidate the business of the partnership. Procedure as to liquidation and distribution of the business of the partnership shall be the same as previously stated for the liquidation of the business in case of the retirement of one of the partners.

IN WITNESS WHEREOF, the parties hereto have hereunto set their hands and seals the day and year first above written.

(Witnesses, if any)	(Signatures)

FORM 4: Partnership Agreement Between Father and Son/Daughter

This Agreement made and entered into this ____ day of _____ ,
19__ , by and between _____ and _____ ,
both of the City of _____ , County of _____ ,
State of _____ , witnesseth:

That the above-named and undersigned parties do hereby form a
partnership for the purpose of carrying on a _____ business, to be a continuation of the _____ business heretofore
owned and operated by _____ , one of the parties hereto, for
which purpose the undersigned have agreed to the following terms and
conditions, to the faithful performance of which they bind themselves each
to the other, their heirs, executors, and administrators:

1. Name and Term: The name and style of the partnership shall
be _____ , and it shall continue until the mutual consent of
the partners to dissolve, subject to the provisions herein set forth.

2. Interest of Partners: The interest in the business shall be held by the
above-named parties in the following proportions, that is to say:

Name	Percentage
_____	_____
_____	_____

3. Management: _____ is to have full and complete
charge of the operation of the business, and shall have the sole authority to
invest funds, purchase equipment, hire, and discharge employees in his
full discretion, and to in all respects manage the conduct and operation of
the business at all times as he may see fit.

4. Distribution of Profits: The net profits arising from the operation of
the business shall be divided between the partners in proportion to their
respective interests herein set out, but shall be payable only at such times
as _____ may in his discretion designate, and he shall have
the right within his discretion to permit the net profits, or any part of the
same, to accumulate and remain in the business until such time as in his
discretion he thinks it proper to pay over the same to the partners in
proportion to their respective interests, and all losses incurred, whether

64

from bad debts, depreciation of goods, or any other cause, and all expenses of the business shall be borne by the partners in the following proportions, that is to say:

Name	*Percentage*
_____	_____
_____	_____

5. Salaries of Partners: _____ shall receive for his services for managing the business the sum of not more than ____ dollars ($____) per month, and such sums so drawn shall be charged as an operating expense and deducted before any division of the profits is made.

6. Purchase of Interest: _____ shall have the right at any time during the existence of this partnership to purchase the interest of _____ upon demand at the then book value of such interest in the business, after deducting any obligation which might then be due and owing by _____ to the partnership, and upon such purchase and payment as aforesaid the interest of _____ in the partnership shall immediately cease and terminate.

7. Disposal of Interest: _____ shall not sell or dispose of his/her interest in the partnership to any third party, but if _____ should desire to dispose of his/her interest in the partnership and retire therefrom, the right is reserved to _____ to purchase the interest of _____ in the partnership at its then book value, less any amount _____ may then owe the partnership.

8. Death of Partner: In the event of the death of either of the partners, the surviving partner shall have the right to purchase from the personal representatives of the deceased partner the interest of such deceased partner in the business at its then book value, such right or option to be exercised by surviving partner within six months from the death of such deceased partner.

9. Books and Accounts: All purchases, sales, transactions, and accounts of the partnership shall be kept in regular books which shall always be open to the inspection of the partners and their legal representatives, and at least once a year a statement shall be prepared showing the net profits of the partnership for the preceding year for the examination of the partners.

Whereas, a verbal agreement was entered into between the undersigned effective as of _____ , 19__ , which verbal agreement contained the provisions and conditions herein set forth, and the partnership has actually been in operation under the verbal agreement since _____ _____ , 19__ , and which verbal agreement has now been reduced to writing as herein set forth, it is understood and agreed with respect to the payment of the net profits arising from the operation of the partnership, the same shall relate back to the ____ day of _____ , 19 __ .

To the faithful performance of this Agreement, the undersigned do hereby bind themselves, their heirs, executors, and administrators.

_____	_____
(Witnesses, if any)	(Signatures)
_____	_____

FORM 5: Partnership Agreement Between Husband and Wife

This Agreement in writing, this day entered into by and between _____
_____ and _____ , husband and wife, witnesseth:

WHEREAS, the parties have engaged in the operation of the _____
_____ , hereinafter mentioned, for a long period of years; and

WHEREAS, certain parts of that business have been conducted in the name of _____ , individually, and certain parts in the name of _____ , individually; and

WHEREAS, certain of the properties used in the operation of the business are not now owned by the parties hereto on an equal basis; and

WHEREAS, it is the desire and intention of the parties to recognize the equal ownership of all of the properties, and the equal responsibility and authority for the management of the business; and

WHEREAS, it is the desire and intention of the parties to enter into this agreement, whereby the equal ownership, responsibility, and authority shall be maintained by the parties on a permanent basis;

NOW, THEREFORE, it is mutually understood and agreed between the parties hereto as follows:

The parties hereto shall be equal partners in the ownership and operation of the _____ conducted under the trade name of _____ all of which business is now being conducted by the parties in the City of _____ , State of _____ , and elsewhere, with the general offices located at _____ , City of _____ , State of _____ .

The assets of the partnership, to be equally owned by the parties, shall include the following:

All office equipment, motor vehicles, supplies, and miscellaneous equipment of all kinds used in the operation of the business.

All accounts receivable of the business and all cash on hand and in banks.

All inventories of furniture and other merchandise on hand at the company offices in _____ , _____ , and elsewhere.

All real estate owned by the undersigned, including the building and lands located at _____ and _____ in the City of _____ , State of _____ .

Appropriate deeds of conveyance shall be executed to effect the equal ownership of the real properties.

The parties shall, from time to time by mutual consent, divide the duties and responsibilities of management of the affairs of the partnership.

The parties shall have an equal interest in the assets of the partnership, and shall share equally in the profits and losses of the business now conducted or hereafter to be conducted by the partnership. It is recognized and agreed that this division of ownership and this division of responsibility and authority embodied in this Agreement is entered into by the parties for the purpose of insuring the stability of the operation of the business and the personal and business affairs of the operation of the business and the personal and business affairs of the parties. In order to accomplish this purpose, it is understood and agreed that this Agreement shall of necessity be permanent, and that it shall not be altered or terminated as long as the undersigned shall remain husband and wife, and that if the parties shall at any time be legally separated or divorced, this Agreement shall thereupon be terminated, and the assets of the partnership divided equally between the parties, and that such division shall constitute a final and complete division of the property and property rights of the undersigned, and shall be in lieu of all other claims between the parties for separate maintenance, alimony, or otherwise.

In the event of the dissolution of the partnership during the lifetime of the parties, and one party desires to continue the operation of the business, such partner shall have the right to purchase the interest of the retiring partner in the assets of the partnership, and to defer the payment of the purchase price therefor over a period of five years from the date of such dissolution.

Witness our signatures, in duplicate, on this the ____ day of _____ _____ , 19__ .

_____   _____
(Witnesses, if any)   (Signatures)

_____   _____

FORM 6: Partnership Agreement for the Operation of Real Estate and Insurance Business

This Agreement, made this ____ day of _____ , 19__ , by and between _____ , hereafter called first party, and _____ _____ , hereafter called the second party, witnesseth:

1. Business: That the second party has acquired an undivided one-half interest in the real estate and insurance business heretofore owned and conducted by the first party, with office and place of business located at _____ , _____ .

2. Firm Name: That the parties hereby agree to continue the operation of that business as partners under the assumed name and style of _____ _____ , the partnership to continue for an indefinite time and until terminated as herein provided or as may be mutually agreed upon.

3. Capital: That the amount of capital contributed to the partnership by the parties is hereby agreed to be the sum of _____ dollars ($ ____) each, and is represented by the following personal property, to wit: (*list each item*)

4. Reserve of Profits: It is hereby agreed that an additional sum of _____ dollars ($ ____) shall be set up and reserved from the profits of the business, and shall become and be a part of the invested capital, it being agreed that not less than ____ percent of the net earnings shall be so reserved until that amount is accumulated.

5. Deposit of Funds: That the capital funds of the partnership, and all other moneys of the partnership, shall be deposited in the name of the partnership in the _____ Bank, and all trust funds shall be deposited in the bank in a separate account, and all such funds, partnership or trust, shall be subject to withdrawal only by check made in the name of the partnership and signed by either partner.

6. Attention of Partners: That each partner shall devote all his time and attention to the business of the partnership, and shall not, directly or indirectly, engage in any other business without the consent of the other partner.

7. Accounts: That full and accurate accounts of the transactions of the partnership shall be kept in proper books, and each partner shall cause to be entered in the books full and accurate accounts of all his transactions on

behalf of the partnership. The books shall be kept at the place of business of the partnership, and each party shall at all times have access to and may inspect and copy any of them.

8. Withdrawals: Each party shall be entitled to draw such amounts and at such times, from the partnership earnings, as shall from time to time be fixed and agreed upon.

9. Annual Account: That at the end of each calendar year, a full and accurate inventory shall be prepared, and the assets, liabilities, and income, both gross and net, shall be ascertained, and the net profits or net losses of the partnership shall be fixed and determined. The net profits or net losses shall be divided equally between the parties hereto, and the account of each shall be credited or debited with his proportionate share thereof.

10. Outside Obligations: That neither party shall, without the written consent of the other, make, execute, deliver, endorse, or guarantee any commercial paper, nor agree to answer for, or indemnify against, any act, debt, default, or miscarriage of any person, partnership, association, or corporation, other than that of the parties hereto.

11. Termination: That the partnership may be terminated by either party upon giving sixty (60) days' notice to the other party of his desire to withdraw, in which event an accounting shall be had and a division of the partnership assets made, provided, however, that the party to whom the notice is given shall have the right to acquire the whole interest of the partnership at a price not to exceed the book value thereof, on such terms as may be agreed upon, and to continue the business under the same business name.

IN WITNESS WHEREOF, we have executed this Agreement this _____ day of _____ , 19__ .

_____   _____
(Witnesses, if any)   (Signatures)

_____   _____

FORM 7: Partnership Agreement Between Inventor and Promoter

This Agreement made this ___ day of _____ , 19__ , between _____ , first party, and _____ , second parties, witnesseth:

WHEREAS, on or about the ___ day of _____ , 19__ , the parties of the second part did apply through _____ , patent attorneys, for letters of patent on a certain device known as the _____ , being Application Number _____ , United States Patent Office; and

WHEREAS, it is the desire of the parties of the second part to procure financial assistance from party of the first part for the purpose of exploiting and promoting the manufacture and sale of the device, and also territorial rights for the promotion and sale of the device when and if patent rights have been issued:

NOW, THEREFORE, it is agreed:

Party of the first part agrees to loan to parties of the second part, from time to time, various sums of money, which sums shall not exceed a total of _____ dollars ($ ___), in the following manner:

In consideration of all and singular the above, parties of the second part do hereby transfer, assign, set over, and sell to party of the first part a ___ percent interest in and to any and all contracts, profits, or benefits derived from the exploitation or sale of the device, or from the sale of any territorial rights appertaining thereto, including the ___ percent interest in and to any and all patent rights now pending in the United States Patent Office, as well as in and to all rights to any improvement thereon hereafter obtained.

It is further agreed by and between the parties hereto that, as advances of funds are made, parties of the second part will, at the option of the party of the first part, secure the same either by promissory notes executed by parties of the second part or by the deposit with party of the first part of contracts for the sale of the device, it being understood that any and all funds or receipts derived from the sale of the device, or from the sale of territorial rights appertaining thereto shall be collected by party of the first part, and the party of the first part shall have the right to retain any and all funds

71

collected on the contracts and to apply the same in repayment of all sums theretofore advanced.

It is further understood and agreed that parties of the second part shall retain full control of the management and operation of the business, subject, however, to the rights of the party of the first part, as hereinabove set forth, it being understood and agreed that it is the desire of all parties hereto to exploit and promote the sale and distribution of the device, and to this end all parties agree to lend their best efforts, it being understood, however, that party of the first part shall not be required to render service other than as herein set forth.

This Agreement shall be binding upon the successors, heirs, executors, administrators, and assigns of the respective parties hereto.

IN WITNESS WHEREOF, the parties have hereunto set their hands the day and year first above written:

_____   _____
(Witnesses, if any)   (Signatures)

_____   _____

FORM 8: Limited Partnership Agreement

We, the undersigned, being desirous of forming a limited partnership, pursuant to the laws of this state do hereby certify:

1. The name of the firm under which said partnership is to be conducted is _____ .

2. The character of the business intended to be transacted by said partnership is as follows: _____ .

3. The location of the principal place of business is to be at _____ .

4. The name and place of residence of each general partner interested in said partnership is as follows: _____ .

5. The name and place of residence of each limited partner interested in said partnership is as follows: _____ .

6. The time at which said partnership is to begin business is _____ , and the time at which said partnership is to end is _____ .

7. The amount of cash and a description of and the agreed value of the other property contributed by each general partner is as follows: _____ .

8. The additional contributions agreed to be made by each general partner and the time at which the event on the happening of which they shall be made is as follows: _____ .

9. The time agreed upon when the contributions of each general partner are to be returned is as follows: _____ .

10. The share of the profits or the other compensation by way of income which each general partner shall receive by reason of his contribution is as follows: _____ .

11. The amount of cash and a description of the agreed value of the other property contributed by each limited partner is as follows: _____ .

12. The additional contributions agreed to be made by each limited partner and the time at which the event on the happening of which they shall be made is as follows: _____ .

13. The share of the profits or the other compensation by way of income which each limited partner shall receive by reason of his contribution is as follows: _____ .

14. The right of a limited partner to substitute an assignee as contributor in his place, and the terms and conditions of the substitution, are as follows: _____ .

15. The right of the partners to admit additional limited partners is as follows: _____ .

16. The right of one or more of the limited partners to priority over other limited partners, as to contributions or as to compensation by way of income, and the nature of such priority are as follows: _____
_____ .

17. The right of the remaining general partner or partners to continue the business on the death, retirement, or insanity of a general partner is as follows: _____ .

18. The right of a limited partner to demand and receive property other than cash in return for his contribution is as follows: _____ .

Date: _____

_____

(Witnesses)

___ _____

_____

_____

_____

General Partner

_____

General Partner

_____

Limited Partner

_____

Limited Partner

FORM 9: Joint Venture for Purchase and Sale of Tract of Land

This Agreement, entered into this ____ day of _____ , 19__ , between _____ , and _____ , witnesseth:

WHEREAS, the parties have purchased and are the owners in common of the following described real estate: _____ ; and

WHEREAS, the property is being purchased under contract for _____ _____ dollars ($ ____) payable as follows: _____ ; and

WHEREAS, _____ is to furnish the money for the purchase, and the legal title of the land is to be held by him;

NOW, THEREFORE, it is hereby mutually agreed by and between the parties hereto, that the proceeds realized from the sale of the real estate when sold, together with the income, if any, from the real estate, after payment of taxes and all costs of every kind and nature, shall be applied as follows: ____ percent to _____ ; ____ percent to _____ _____ ; and should any loss be incurred by reason of the purchase of the real estate, such loss shall be borne ____ percent by _____ , and ____ percent by _____ .

It is further agreed that the best efforts shall be made by all parties hereto, to accomplish the sale of the land, and when a profit of ____ percent or more can be obtained, parties hereto shall agree to a sale. Unless profits from sales, or income from the property, shall be sufficient to carry taxes, interest and charges, and insurance at the end of ____ years from this date and thereafter, it is understood that _____ will carry ____ percent, and _____ will carry ____ percent of such sums after the ____ year period has expired.

IN WITNESS WHEREOF, we have executed this Agreement this ____ day of _____ , 19__ .

_____   _____
(Witnesses, if any)   (Signatures)

_____   _____

FORM 10: Joint Venture for Construction of Apartment

This Agreement made the ____ day of _____ , 19__ , by and between _____ of the first part, and _____ of the second part, witnesseth:

WHEREAS, first party is the owner in fee simple of the following described property: _____ ; and

WHEREAS, the first party is about to begin the erection of an apartment house thereon, hereafter referred to as the improvements;

NOW, THEREFORE, in consideration of the premises and of the agreements therein, and for other good and valuable considerations, the receipt whereof is hereby confessed and acknowledged, it is agreed by and between the parties as follows:

Second party is to furnish all plans and specifications and pay all charges for the superintendency necessary in the erection of the improvements.

On the completion of the improvements by the first party, the building is to be offered for sale at the best price obtainable, and when sold, the parties hereto are to participate equally in the sale price, after first party has deducted the cost of the lot and the net cost of the improvements.

In the event the improvements are not sold forthwith after completion, then the premises are to be rented, and the net income of the improvements and rentals is to be applied to a sinking fund controlled by both parties to this Agreement, and it is to be applied from time to time as the same matures on taxes, expenses, debts, and claims of every kind and nature against the premises until the same is completely paid out and the property stands free and clear of all taxes, liens, encumbrances, debts, or claims of any kind or nature whatsoever.

And it is agreed that there shall be no division of any moneys received from such income and rentals until the same is completely paid for, as herein in this paragraph provided, except upon the written consent, signed by both of the parties hereto, and the agreement of division must be signed in duplicate and attached to the duplicate copies of this Agreement.

It is understood and agreed that the term "net income" referred to in the preceding paragraph hereof means and is defined as that income or rentals from the improvements which will remain after deductions are made for general taxes, interest charged on loans outstanding against the improvements, insurance, water, rent, and cost of upkeep of the improvements.

It is further understood that the parties hereto will necessarily expend various and sundry items of moneys for legal services, payment of special taxes and incidentals, and it is agreed that each party is to keep a strict account and render to the other itemized statements of such expenditures and receipts therefor, and that the respective amounts are to be charged against the gross income of the premises at the completion thereof, and each party is to be reimbursed for all expenditures so made.

Time is of the essence hereof in every particular, and the covenants and agreements herein shall be binding upon and insure to the benefits of the heirs, executors, administrators, and assigns of the respective parties hereto.

IN WITNESS WHEREOF, we have hereunto signed this Agreement this ____ day of _____ , 19__ .

_____   _____
(Witnesses, if any)   (Signatures)

_____   _____

FORM 11: Sale of Partnership Interest to Copartners

This Agreement made and entered into this ____ day of _____ ____ , 19__ , by and between _____ and _____ , witness and agree:

WHEREAS, the above-named parties are at present engaged in the business known as _____ , as partners under a certain agreement in writing, dated _____ , 19__ , and

WHEREAS, _____ has proposed to buy out the interest of _____ in said partnership, for the sum of _____ ____ dollars, and _____ has agreed to sell to _____ ____ his interest in said partnership for said amount if the conditions hereinafter stated are complied with.

IT IS HEREBY AGREED AS FOLLOWS:

1. _____ , for and in consideration of the sum of _____ _____ dollars, paid to him by _____ , receipt of which is hereby acknowledged, does hereby assign, sell, and transfer unto ____ _____ , all of his interest in and to said partnership business, including his interest in all of the furniture, equipment, and furnishings of said business, stock of merchandise of said business, accounts receivable of said business, moneys in said business, and all of his right, title, and interest in and to any and all of the assets of whatsoever kind or nature, of the _____ company.

2. It is agreed that _____ shall and does assume and agree to pay all of the outstanding debts and obligations of the said partnership business, and to perform all of the covenants of the leases on the said premises, and to perform all other outstanding contracts and agreements required to be performed by said partnership; and _____ agrees to save and hold harmless _____ against any claim or claims that may arise by reason of the aforesaid debts, obligations, or covenants, or of any other claims, except those mentioned in the following paragraph.

3. _____ hereby warrants and represents that he has incurred no debts, nor contracted any obligations, nor has he incurred any liability in the name of the partnership, or for which the partnership would be liable, other than such debts, obligations, or liabilities as are

disclosed in the books of the partnership, or of which he has advised _____ ; and _____ agrees to save and hold harmless _____ on account of any claims that may be made against said partnership because of any debts, obligations, or liabilities which _____ incurred in the name of the partnership or which the partnership has become liable for on account of any act of _____ , as to which _____ has failed or neglected to inform _____ .

4. _____ agrees to prepare Federal Partnership Income Tax Returns for the partnership business from _____ , 19__ to this date, and to supply _____ with a copy thereof. It is agreed that each of the parties hereto shall pay their individual income taxes on the income received from said partnership business.

5. All other tax obligations (including occupational taxes, personal property taxes, and various municipal licensing fees) shall be considered as obligations of the partnership, and are hereby assumed by _____ .

6. It is agreed that the partnership heretofore existing between the parties hereto be, and the same is, hereby dissolved, and that this Agreement constitutes a full and complete accounting and liquidation of said partnership business, and, excepting as herein otherwise provided, _____ acknowledges that he has no claim or demand of whatsoever kind or nature against _____ , and, except as herein otherwise provided, _____ acknowledges that he has no claim or demand of whatsoever kind or nature against _____ .

IN WITNESS WHEREOF, the parties hereto have signed this Agreement.

_____   _____
(Witnesses, if any)   (Signatures)

_____   _____

FORM 12: Dissolution Agreement

This Agreement made this ____ day of _____ , 19__ , by and between _____ and _____ , witness and agree:

That whereas, the parties to this agreement have heretofore conducted a partnership under the firm name and style of _____ ; and

WHEREAS, _____ is desirous of withdrawing from said partnership and both the parties thereto have agreed and do agree that said partnership shall be dissolved and terminated; and

WHEREAS, _____ has this day conveyed to _____ _____ all his interest in the real estate and certain of the personal property heretofore owned by said partnership upon the agreement that the assets of said partnership shall be promptly liquidated and said partnership terminated and closed.

NOW, THEREFORE, it is mutually agreed that the partnership heretofore existing between the parties to this Agreement, shall be liquidated and dissolved at as early a date as the same can be practically accomplished without loss to the parties in interest and the net assets realized, after paying all debts and expenses of liquidating the assets and caring for the property in the partnership, shall be divided equally between the parties hereto.

IN WITNESS WHEREOF, the parties hereto have signed this Agreement.

_____   _____
(Witnesses, if any)   (Signatures)

_____   _____

FORM 13: Notice of Dissolution

Notice is hereby given that the partnership heretofore existing between
_____ and _____ , under the fictitious name
and style of _____ Company, located at _____ ,
_____ , _____ , was dissolved by mutual
consent, on the ____ day of ____ , 19__ .
_____ has withdrawn from and has ceased to be associated in the carrying on of said business, and _____ will
hereafter carry on said business and he is entitled to all of the assets,
including all debts due to said partnership, and has assumed and will pay
all outstanding business obligations of _____ Company
heretofore and hereafter incurred.

_____   _____

                               (Signatures)

_____   _____

FORM 14: Notice under Fictitious Name Law

Notice is hereby given that the undersigned desiring to engage in
business at _____ under the name of _____
Company, intend to register the said name with the Clerk and Recorder
of _____ County.

_____   _____

Date   (Signatures)

_____   _____

81

FORM 15: Buy and Sell Agreement Between Two Parties

Agreement made this _____ day of _____ , 19___ , between
_____ , who resides at _____ , and _____
_____ , who resides at _____ .

_____ and _____ are partners doing business in the partnership known as _____ . The interest of each partner in said partnership is set forth as follows:

_____ has _____ percent
_____ has _____ percent

The purpose of this Agreement is to provide for the purchase of the decedent's interest in said partnership by the survivor.

It is, therefore, mutually agreed by _____ and _____
_____ as follows:

1. Neither _____ nor _____ shall during their joint lives, assign, encumber, or dispose of any portion of their respective partnership interests in the _____ Company, by sale or otherwise, without the written consent of the other partner.

2. Upon the death of either partner, the survivor shall purchase, and the estate of the decedent shall sell, the partnership interest then owned by the partner who is first to die. The purchase price of such interest shall be computed in accordance with the provisions of paragraph 3 of this Agreement.

3. Unless and until changed as hereinafter provided, the total value of _____ , for the purpose of determining the purchase price to be paid for the interest of a deceased partner, shall be _____ dollars, and the value of each partner's interest in said partnership shall be as follows:

The interest of _____ shall be _____ dollars
The interest of _____ shall be _____ dollars

(a) The said purchase price includes an amount mutually agreed upon as representing the goodwill of the partnership as a going concern.

(b) Within _____ days following the end of each fiscal year, _____
_____ and _____ shall redetermine the value of said partnership and their respective interests therein. Such values

shall be endorsed on Schedule A, attached hereto. If _____ and _____ fail to determine said values for a particular year, the last previously stipulated values shall control, except that if no valuation is agreed upon for two consecutive years, the value of a partner's interest shall be determined by the independent, certified public accountant regularly retained by the partnership for the auditing of its books. If there is no such public accountant available, or if he fails to make a determination of such valuation, then the value shall be determined by any other accountant who may be selected by mutual agreement of the surviving partner, and the representative of the deceased partner.

(c) The surviving partner shall be entitled to all the profits of the business and suffer all the losses arising between the date of death of the deceased partner and the consummation of the sale of the interest of the deceased partner.

4. The purchase price shall be payable as follows: Not less than _____ _____ dollars in cash, or the entire purchase price in cash if less than said amount, and if any balance of the purchase price remains unpaid, it shall be covered by a series of promissory notes of equal amounts payable to the order of the executors or administrators of the deceased partner, the first note maturing in _____ , the second in _____ , and the final one in _____ , with interest on each note at the rate of ____ percent per annum, to be paid when each promissory note comes due on the unpaid balance. The surviving partner may elect to pay more than the specified amount in cash, may elect to have notes for a shorter period, and may pay any note in advance of its due date. The executors or administrators of the seller may agree to more liberal terms, such as a smaller amount of the purchase in cash, or notes for a longer period, or at a lower rate of interest, and may extend notes or waive any defaults, if they determine any such action to the best interest of the estate and the heirs and legatees of the deceased partner.

5. If notes are given in partial payment of the agreed purchase price, they shall be secured by a chattel mortgage on the tangible assets of the partnership of a value of ____ times the amount of the notes. All notes of the surviving partner shall forthwith fall due in event of default in payment of interest or principal of any note of said surviving partner.

6. The surviving partner shall pay and discharge all liabilities of the partnership existing at the date of the deceased partner's death, and shall save and keep the estate of the deceased partner free and relieved from any and all liability, either to the partnership or to any of the creditors of the partnership, and shall indemnify the deceased partner's estate against all costs, losses, and damages sustained or paid by the representatives of the estate in respect of partnership liabilities.

7. The surviving partner and the executors or administrators of the deceased partner shall make, execute, and deliver any document necessary to transfer ownership of the partnership assets and to carry out this Agreement.

8. This Agreement may be altered, amended, or terminated by a writing by both partners.

9. This Agreement shall terminate on the occurrence of any of the following events:

    (a) Bankruptcy, receivership, or dissolution of the partnership;

    (b) Bankruptcy, or insolvency of either partner;

    (c) Death of both partners simultaneously or within a period of thirty days;

    (d) Termination of the partnership business.

10. This Agreement shall be binding upon the partners, their heirs, legal representatives, successors, and assigns.

IN WITNESS WHEREOF, the parties hereto have executed this Agreement this _____ day of _____ , 19__ .

_____	_____
(Witnesses, if any)	(Signatures)
_____	_____

SCHEDULE A—Endorsements

Pursuant to Article 3 of this Agreement, the parties do hereby determine that the total value of the partnership business as of this _____ day of _____ , 19__ , and the value of each partner's respective interest is: _____

_____

FORM 16: Alternative, Additional, and Supplemental Provisions for Partnership Agreements

There may be some occasions where additional provisions are desirable in an agreement or where further facts or details are needed to make the intention of the parties clear. You should use your discretion in determining whether, how, and to what extent, you utilize these clauses or parts of them to make your agreement complete. You should be careful not to use clauses on the same subject matter which may be inconsistent, contradictory, or indefinite.

Form 16.01: Purpose Clauses

Sample 1:

The purpose of the partnership shall be the buying, selling, and exchanging of _____ and the doing of all things necessary and incidental thereto.

Sample 2:

The partnership shall be for the purpose of carrying on the business of manufacturing and selling of _____ and other items related thereto of whatsoever kind or character.

Sample 3:

The business of the partnership shall be as follows:

(1) To establish, maintain, conduct, and engage in the business of building and manufacturing of _____ .

(2) To establish, maintain, conduct, and engage in the business of designing, developing, and drafting of plans, specifications, and designs for _____ .

(3) To manufacture, build, and assemble such articles as _____ _____ .

(4) To buy, sell, hold, and convey such equipment, machinery, fixtures, and other personal property as may be necessary for the operation of the business herein contemplated by this partnership agreement.

Form 16.02: Conduct of Business and Authority of Partners

Sample 1:

Equal Authority to Conduct Business: Each partner shall have an equal right in the management of the partnership business, and a decision by the majority shall be binding upon the partnership. However, no partner shall contract in the name and on the credit of the partnership in excess of _____ dollars without the consent of all the partners.

Sample 2:

Management: _____ shall be the manager of said partnership and shall be authorized to sign all notes, checks, drafts, and other obligations and to execute all papers, under seal or otherwise. Further, he shall be in full charge of all business operations of said partnership for the purpose of carrying out the provisions of this Agreement. All decisions affecting the policy and management of the partnership, including the drawing accounts and compensation of partners and the control of employment, compensation, and discharge of employees shall be made on behalf of the partnership upon the approval of a majority of the partners.

Sample 3:

Meetings of Partners: For the purpose of discussing matters of general interest to the partnership, together with the conduct of its business, partners shall meet each ____ of each week, at ____ o'clock in the morning, or at such other time agreed upon by a majority of the partners. All meetings shall be decided by a majority vote of the partners, except that no change shall be made in the nature or scope of the partnership business, nor shall any act be done which would make it impossible to carry out the ordinary business of the partnership business, nor shall any change be made in this partnership agreement except with the consent of all the partners.

Form 16.03: Deposit of Money

All moneys which shall from time to time be received for or on account of said partnership, not required for current expenses, shall be deposited immediately in the bank for the time being dealt with by the partnership, in the same drafts, checks, bills, or cash in which the same are received, and all disbursements for or on account of the partnership shall be made by check on such bank.

Form 16.04: Expense Accounts

Each partner shall be entitled to an expense account of not to exceed _____ dollars per week, of his actual, reasonable, and necessary expenses, incurred for and in behalf of the firm, but shall keep an itemized account thereof, which account shall only bind the other members thereof, when approved in writing by at least a majority of the partners. All such accounts shall be filed, after such approval, and kept for a period of at least one year after such approval.

Form 16.05: Time to Be Devoted to Firm

Each partner shall devote his whole time and attention to the partnership business, and diligently and faithfully employ himself therein, and carry on the same to the greatest advantage of the partnership.

Form 16.06: Bond

Each member of this partnership shall enter into a bond in the sum of _____ dollars, satisfactory to all of his partners hereunder, to the effect that he shall fully account to the said partnership for all property of the said firm which shall come to his possession, and that he will turn the same over to said firm.

Form 16.07: Vacations

Each partner shall be entitled to _____ weeks' vacation in each year. In the first year of the partnership, the said _____ shall have the first choice of the time at which he shall take his vacation, and in all succeeding years the choice shall be made by the partners alternately.

Form 16.08: Engaging in Other Business

No partner shall, during the continuance of the partnership, carry on or be concerned or interested, directly or indirectly, in the same kind of business as that carried on by said partnership, nor be engaged in or undertake any other trade, or business, without the consent in writing of the other partners or partner.

Form 16.09: Managing Partner

The said _____ shall be the manager of the said business, and shall be paid for his services as manager the annual sum of _____ _____ dollars before any division of profits is made, and in addition thereto his share of the profits, by equal quarterly payments, the first salary payment to be made on the _____ day of _____ , 19__ .

Form 16.10: Devotion to Business

Sample 1:

It is agreed by the parties to this Agreement, that at all times during the continuance of their partnership, they and each of them will give their attention and attendance, and to the utmost of their skill and power will exert themselves for their joint interest, profit, benefit, and advantage.

Sample 2:

It is agreed by and between the parties hereto, that at all times during the continuance of the partnership, each partner shall give reasonable time, attention, and attendance to, and use reasonable endeavors in, the business of the partnership, and shall, with reasonable skill and power, exert himself for the joint interest, profit, and advantage of the partnership.

Form 16.11: Maintenance and Availability of Records

Sample 1:

Each of the partners may have access at all times to the books, papers, and records of the partnership, and may have them audited and examined by auditors, accountants, or attorneys at the sole and entire expense of the partner desiring the audit or examination.

Sample 2:

Books of accounts shall be kept and entries made therein of all moneys, goods, effects, debts, sales, purchases, receipts, payments, and all other writings belonging to the said partnership, shall be kept where the business of the partnership shall be carried on, and shall be at all times open to the examination of each partner.

Sample 3:

It is understood and agreed that there shall be kept at all times a complete set of books of account wherein there shall be entered any and all records and transactions of said business and that every month from the date hereof after the payment of all expenses of said partnership, including interest on the capital invested herein, and also at the expiration or other termination hereof, and books shall be balanced and a balance sheet shall be delivered to each partner showing the profits or losses from said partnership, as the same shall have been accurately ascertained, and such profits shall be shared by and divided between and credited to such losses borne by and charged to said partners in the proportions hereinabove set forth, and thereupon each partner shall be permitted to draw out his share of the profits, if any, so credited.

Form 16.12: Management by Individual Partner

It is understood and agreed by and between the said partners that _____ shall be, and is from this date on, made the general manager of said partnership, that he shall be in full charge of all business operations of said partnership, and that he shall have the full right to conduct the business of said partnership in such manner as he may desire, including the selling of any and all of the partnership assets and the purchasing of such other property as he may desire in the name of the partnership together with the right to borrow such money as he may deem necessary to carry on said business.

Form 16.13: Method of Resolving Differences

In the event of any misunderstanding between the partners concerning the matter of conducting and carrying on said business, the partners shall adjust the same between themselves. It is understood, however, in this connection that the decision of the general manager and one other partner hereto shall determine any question which may arise between them and in the event that any one or more of said partners should be dissatisfied with such decision, then they shall have the right as given them by the laws of the State of _____ to bring proceedings in court for the purpose of either dissolving the said partnership or obtaining such relief as they are entitled to under the terms of this partnership agreement.

Form 16.14: Arbitration of Disputes

Sample 1:

If any disagreement shall arise between the partners in respect to the conduct of the business of the partnership, or its dissolution, or in respect to any other cause, matter, or thing whatsoever not otherwise provided for in the aforesaid partnership agreement, the same shall be decided and determined by one arbitrator, to wit: _____ , and the decision of said arbitrator shall be binding and conclusive on the parties hereto.

Sample 2:

In the event that any dispute should arise concerning any of the terms, covenants, or conditions of this Agreement, or with respect to the enforcement thereof, or with respect to any dissolution or liquidation of the partnership, or with respect to any matter affecting the operation and conduct of the business of the partnership, such dispute shall be disposed of by arbitration by submitting the same to the American Arbitration Association in accordance with the rules and regulations of that associa-

tion then obtaining, and in accordance with the laws of the State of
_____ .

Form 16.15: Deposit and Withdrawal of Funds

Partnership moneys received from any and all sources shall be deposited
in the name of the _____ Company in the _____
Bank, and shall be withdrawn therefrom only by check drawn and signed
by _____ .

Form 16.16: Prohibition Against Commingling

All trust and other similar funds shall be deposited in another fund in
the firm's name in another bank or trust company, and shall not be
mingled with other moneys of the firm.

Form 16.17: Control of Majority of Partners

The vote of a majority of the partners shall control any question that
may come up for decision unless otherwise provided herein.

Form 16.18: Right to Expel Partner

The right to terminate the interest of any one of the partners is hereby
vested in the other partners for any cause which in their discretion seems to
be reasonable, and the interests set forth hereinafter are accepted with this
express condition and limitation.

Form 16.19: Authority to Sign Checks and Written Instruments

It is understood and agreed that all checks to be drawn in the regular
course of business of the firm shall be signed by _____ .
Checks of the firm shall be used only for the firm business and no account
or charge against any of the partners shall be paid with a firm check. In the
event it becomes necessary to borrow money and to execute any bills, notes,

contracts, or agreements binding the firm or pledging the firm credit, the same must be executed by _____ .

Form 16.20: Restrictions on Powers of Partners

No partner shall, without the written consent of the others, enter into any bond or become an endorser or surety for any person, or knowingly cause or suffer to be done anything whereby the partnership property may be seized, attached, or taken on execution or endangered, nor shall such partner assign, mortgage, or charge his share of the assets of profits of the partnership, or any part of said share, or draw, accept, or endorse any bill of exchange or promissory note on account of the partnership.

Form 16.21: Requirement of Countersignature of Partner

No checks shall be drawn or vouchers issued unless signed by at least two parties to this Agreement.

Form 16.22: Requirements of Mutual Assent to Guaranties

None of the partners, during the continuance of this partnership, shall assume any liability for another or others, by means of endorsement or of becoming guarantor or surety, without first obtaining the consent of the other thereto in writing.

Form 16.23: Covenant of Good Faith

Each of the parties hereto shall diligently employ himself in the business of said partnership, and be faithful to the other in all transactions relating to the same, and give, whenever required, a true account of all business transactions arising out of, or connected with, the conduct of the partnership, and neither of the parties shall engage in any business except that of the said partnership or on account thereof, and neither shall, without the written consent of the other, employ either the capital or credit of the partnership in any other than partnership business.

Form 16.24: Indemnification Against Partner's Separate Debts

Sample 1:

Neither party shall do or suffer to be done anything whereby the capital or the property of the partnership may be attached or taken in execution, and each partner shall punctually pay his separate debts and indemnify the other partners and the capital and property of the partnership against the same.

Sample 2:

Each partner shall promptly pay his debts, and keep indemnified the other partners, and the stock-in-trade, capital, and property of the partnership, against the same, and all expenses on account thereof.

Sample 3:

Each partner shall at all times duly and punctually pay and discharge his separate and private debts and engagements whether present or future and keep indemnified therefrom and from all actions, claims, and demands in respect thereof, the partnership property.

Form 16.25: Restriction on Engaging in Other Enterprises

Neither of the partners shall, during the term, use the trade or business of the firm, as aforesaid, for his private benefit or advantage; but shall, at all times, do his best by all lawful means to the utmost of his skill and power, for the joint interest, profit, benefit, and advantage of the firm.

Form 16.26: Partnership Right to Patents and Trade Secrets

Any ideas that may be the subject of application for letters patent and trade secrets or formulas discovered by either of the parties during the course of the partnership shall become partnership property.

Form 16.27: Admission of Sons or Daughters into Firm

Either of said partners may at any time nominate a son/daughter, being of the age of twenty-one years or more, to succeed to his/her share in the partnership and the capital and future profits thereof; and upon signing a proper written contract respecting the admission of a new partner, every such son/daughter shall be and become a partner in the partnership concern in the place, and in respect of the share and interest, of his/her father/mother therein, and be entitled thereto upon the same terms and conditions, and under the subject to the same advantages, regulations, and agreements, in all respects and in the same manner, as the father/mother would have been entitled to if he/she had remained a partner, or as near thereto as the difference of circumstances will permit.

3

Rights and Duties Among Partners

Relations of Partners among Themselves

The Uniform Partnership Act sets out in considerable detail the rules determining the rights and duties of partners toward each other. But you will remember that these rights and duties may be altered by agreement among the partners. Among the rights specifically set out in the Uniform Act are the *rights of each partner:*

1. to share equally in the profits of the firm,
2. to receive repayment of his contribution,
3. to receive indemnification for payments made on behalf of the firm,
4. to receive interest on advances and, under certain circumstances, on capital contributions,
5. to share in the management and conduct of the business,
6. to have access to the firm books, and
7. to have a formal account of partnership affairs.

These rights are complemented by certain *duties:*

1. to contribute toward losses sustained by the firm,
2. to work for the partnership without remuneration,

3. to submit to a majority vote when differences arise among the partners as to the conduct of the firm business,
4. to disclose to other partners any information a partner has regarding partnership matters, and
5. to account to the firm for any profit derived by a partner from any partnership transaction or from the use of partnership property.

Although not stated in so many words in the Uniform Act, one of the principal obligations of partners toward each other is to exercise the utmost good faith and maintain the highest integrity in dealing with each other.

Relations of Partner to the Partnership

The terms of a partnership agreement may expressly regulate the duty of the partners to render services to the firm. By these terms, partners often agree to exert themselves during the continuance of the partnership for their mutual interest, profit, and advantage. In the absence of an agreement to the contrary, each partner is required to give to the firm all of his or her time, skill, and ability. It is also his or her duty to use his or her knowledge, skill, and diligence for the promotion of the common benefit of the business.

As stated in the Uniform Act, no partner is entitled to remuneration for acting in the partnership business, unless otherwise agreed by the partners. It goes on to state that a surviving partner is entitled to reasonable compensation for his or her services in winding up the partnership affairs. It is recognized that in managing partnership affairs, each partner is, in effect, taking care of his or her own interest or managing his or her own business, and is merely performing his or her own duties and obligations growing out of his or her role as a partner. For the rendition of such services he or she is not, in the absence of a contract, express or implied, entitled to compensation beyond his or her share of the profits.

The rule that partners have a fiduciary duty to other partners extends to the partnership and each partner has the obligation of maintaining the utmost good faith and integrity in his or her dealings with the partnership and the partnership affairs. It is a fundamental characteristic of the partnership that the relation existing between the partners is one of trust and confidence when dealing with each other in relation to partnership matters. Each partner is, in one sense, a trustee. The same rules and tests are applied to the conduct of partners as are ordinarily applicable to trustees and agents.

In applying these general statements, each partner has a right to know all that the others know about their business matters. Each is required to make full disclosure of all material facts within his or her knowledge in any way relating to the partnership affairs. One partner may not deceive another partner by the concealment of material facts. A partner, in acting for the partnership, must consult his or her partners in every important activity of the partnership affairs, in the absence of special circumstances excusing him or her from so doing.

The Uniform Act reinforces the above rules by providing that partners must render on demand true and full information of all things affecting the partnership to any partner or the legal representative of any deceased partner or any partner under legal disability. The duty imposed by the Uniform Act is owed by all partners, but the standard of rigid, fair dealing required of a managing partner to the inactive partners is especially high.

Power of Partners

The functions, rights, and duties of partners are based primarily on the principles of agency. In fact, the law of partnership is a branch of the law of agency, and it is universally recognized that the liability of one partner for the acts of his copartners is founded on principles of agency. It follows that every partner, apart from any special powers conferred on him by the partnership agreement, is not only a principal, but is also, for all purposes within the scope and objects of the partnership, a general and authorized agent of the firm, and the agent of all the partners. This is the fundamental basis upon which you may be held liable and responsible for acts of your partners.

A partner virtually acts as principal for himself or herself and as agent for his or her partners, and for the partnership. During the existence of a partnership, therefore, each member is deemed to be authorized to transact the whole business for the firm, his or her acts being treated as the acts of all. If the partner has the requisite authority, he or she binds the partnership whether he or she acts in its name or his or her own name. The law presumes there is liability for a transaction entered into by a partner acting apparently within the scope of his or her authority. Evidence which might prove favorable for the other members of the partnership may include a showing that credit was given to the individual partner alone, or that it was known that such partner acted fraudulently or without the authority and consent of his or her partners, or any other facts to demonstrate a lack of liability.

Under the Uniform Act, as well as at common law, an individual partner can by his or her acts bind the partnership by entering into contracts with third parties within the limits allowed by the partnership agreement. This should encourage all partners to have a full and complete partnership agreement in writing.

4

Property Rights of Partners

Partnership Property

All property originally brought into the partnership stock or subsequently acquired by purchase or otherwise, on account of the partnership, is partnership property, and unless the contrary intention appears, property acquired with partnership funds is property of the partnership. Real estate may be acquired in the firm name and may be conveyed in the partnership name.

In contrast to its regulation of sales of real property, the Uniform Act does not specifically deal with sales of personal property. At common law dealing in personal property was also much less circumscribed than dealing in realty since personal property was generally recognized as being the property of the firm and not of individual partners.

Individual Rights of Partners in Partnership

The specific property rights of an individual partner in the partnership property, under the Uniform Act, include (1) his or her rights in specific partnership property, (2) his or her interest in the partnership, and (3) his or her right to participate in the management of the business of the partnership. His or her interest in the partnership, by whatever name it may be called, is personal property. A partner is coowner with his or her partners of specific partnership property holding as a tenant in partnership. The nature, incidents, and characteristics of this tenancy in partnership are not always clear; however, the Uniform Act sets out, in some detail, a description of the property right.

In all discussions about the Uniform Act, it is emphasized that the Act has been adopted in virtually all states in whole or in part, and that its rules apply in most instances only if there is not a written partnership agreement establishing some other specific arrangement.

5

Liability of Partnership to Third Parties

Civil Liability

Since the rights and duties of partners are generally measured by the rules applicable to the agency relationship, the liability of one partner for the acts of his or her partners is based on the rule that each one is an agent of every other. The Uniform Act prescribes the nature of the liability. With respect for the firm's liability for acts performed in its name and within the scope of its business, the partners are jointly liable for all debts and obligations of the partnership. Each partner is bound by admissions or representations made by any partner regarding partnership affairs. Such liability also extends to negligence, wrongful acts, and breach of trust by partners acting within the scope of the partnership business. This exposure to liability is the primary objection to conducting a business through a partnership arrangement.

Criminal Liability

A partnership can violate a criminal statute apart from the participation and knowledge of the partners as individuals, but the conviction of a partnership cannot be used to punish the individual partners, who might be completely free of personal guilt. The criminal conviction of a partnership as an entity can lead only to a fine levied on the firm's assets. The argument has been made that the words "knowingly" and "willfully" in a criminal statute eliminate partnership from the coverage of such statutes because a partnership, as opposed to its individual partners, cannot act knowingly and willfully. The United States Supreme Court has rejected this argument holding that, while partnerships as well as corporations and other associations cannot so act, it is elementary that such impersonal entities can be guilty of knowing or willful violations of regulatory statutes through the acts of its agents. The courts reasoned that, if the partnership itself obtains the fruits of the violations which are committed knowingly by agents of the firm in the scope of their employment, the business entity cannot be left free to break the law merely because its owners, that is, the partners, do not personally participate in the legal activity.

The Uniform Act provides that where any wrongful act of any partner acting in the ordinary course of business causes loss or injury to any nonpartner, or where, as a result, "any penalty is incurred," the partnership is then liable to the same extent as the individual partner. Consequently, a usury penalty may be imposed against a partnership engaged in the loan business or extending credit.

A partnership engaged in a lawful enterprise generally will not cause one partner to be liable for the intentional criminal act of another. There may be liability, however, if unlawful acts are done with knowledge and consent of the partners. In other words, while the partnership, as an entity, can be held for the criminal acts of its agents, individual partners cannot be convicted of willfully violating a criminal law without a showing that they had knowledge of the criminal act of their agent, or that they received and appropriated the benefit of the act. But where a partner willfully participates in a violation of law, the fact that he, as well as the partnership, is indicted does not constitute a violation of the constitutional prohibition against double jeopardy.

Where guilty intent is an element of a crime, partners who do not participate in a criminal act will not be held liable. Conversely, if all the partners participate in a criminal act, all are guilty.

6

Dissolution of Partnership and Winding Up of Partnership Business

Although courts and lawyers are not always precise in distinguishing among the various terms which apply to that process which leads to the final settlement of all partnership affairs, the authors of the Uniform Act suggest the following delineation: Dissolution designates that point in time when the partners cease to carry on the business together; winding up (often called liquidation) is the process of settling partnership affairs after dissolution; and termination is the point in time when all the partnership affairs are wound up.

Dissolution of Partnership

The Uniform Act defines dissolution as the change in the relation of the partners caused by any partner ceasing to be associated in the carrying on of the business. Dissolution is not in itself a termination of the partnership or of the rights and powers of partners, for many of these persist during the winding up process. Rather, the term is descriptive of that change in the partnership relation which ultimately results in its termination.

107

Dissolution is caused either by operation of law or by judicial decree. Where the Uniform Act is in effect, the dissolution of a partnership can only be brought about as provided by the Act. However, the courts have recognized that dissolution may take place under certain circumstances not specifically enumerated in the Act. For example, the admission or withdrawal of a partner from the firm has been held to result in dissolution.

The dissolution of a partnership can be caused or required by any number of things, including the following: by operation of law, termination of term or purpose, by will of one partner, by mutual consent, the admission of a new partner, the withdrawal or retirement of a partner, expulsion or exclusion of a partner, assignment of a partner's interest in the partnership, assignment of a partner's property rights, sale or transfer of firm effects, changes in personal status of partners, bankruptcy or insolvency, and many others.

Winding Up of Business

Winding up means the administration of assets for the purpose of terminating the business and discharging the obligations of the partnership to its members. But while the provision of the Uniform Act relating to the application of partnership property on dissolution is concerned with a discontinuance of the day-to-day business, it does not forbid other methods of winding up a partnership. For example, a provision for withdrawal of a partner may be considered a type of winding up of a partnership without the necessity of discontinuing the daily business.

The Uniform Act provides that unless otherwise agreed, the partners who have not wrongfully dissolved the partnership, or the legal representative of the last surviving partner, if not bankrupt, have the right to wind up the partnership affairs. Where dissolution is caused by the bankruptcy of a partner, the power to wind up is vested in the nonbankrupt partner unless there is a different agreement. Any partner, his legal representative, or his assignee, upon dissolution, may file court action to obtain winding up under court jurisdiction.

Where a partnership is ended by mutual consent or by the expiration of its term, the right to wind up is vested in all the partners. In that case, each partner is under a duty to liquidate partnership affairs, which would include the performance of existing contracts, the collection of debts or claims due the firm, and the payment of firm debts.

The partners who have the right to wind up may agree that one or more of them shall act as liquidating partners. It requires no express authority to act as a liquidating partner after active operations of the firm have ceased, or after its dissolution. If a partner so acts with the knowledge of the other partners, their permission may be presumed. The partner who remains in charge of the business during the winding up period occupies a fiduciary relationship to the other partners until the winding up of the partnership affairs is complete. If the partners cannot agree as to who shall wind up, a receiver may be appointed by the court.

Accounting

One of the ordinary duties of partners is to keep true and correct books showing the firm accounts, such books being at all times open to the inspection of all the members of the firm. This duty primarily rests on the managing or active partner, and he or she cannot defeat the rights of his or her partner to a settlement and proper distribution of the assets by failing to keep the accounts. In fact, the managing partner will be held to strict proof of the items of his or her accounts. In determining whether the managing partner has properly performed the proper duties in keeping accounts, the court may consider the nature of the business, the intellectual ability of the partners, and the place of condition under which the work is to be performed.

According to the Uniform Act the partnership book shall be kept, subject to any agreement between the partners, at the principal place of business of the partnership, and every partner shall at all times have access to and may inspect and copy any of them. This provision refs to an active partnership. When a partnership is dissolved, the firm books and records belong to all of the partners.

Application of Assets to Liabilities
Ranking of Liabilities

In settling accounts between partners after dissolution, the Uniform Act states that the liabilities of the partnership rank in payment as follows:

1. those owed to creditors other than partners;
2. those owed to partners other than for capital and profits;
3. those owed to partners in respect of capital; and
4. those owed to partners in respect of profits.

These statutory rules for distribution of assets are applicable only in the absence of an agreement between the partners specifying some other method of distribution.

After the payment of liabilities, the surplus may be applied to the payment of the net amount owed to the partners. When a partner leaves the firm voluntarily, or involuntarily, without assigning his interest to the other partners or agreeing to continuation of the business, he or she is entitled to receive an amount equal to the value of his or her interest at dissolution. The same rule applies when a partner dies so that his or her representative may have the value of the deceased's interest at the date of dissolution.

Rights of Firm Creditors

It is clear that both under the Uniform Act and under the doctrine of marshalling of assets, the first rank in order of payment is for liabilities owed to creditors other than the partners. All firm debts must be paid before any partner is entitled to any part of the firm assets. Each partner has the right to have the partnership property applied to the payment or security for the payment of partnership debts in order to relieve him or her from personal liability. Upon the death of a partner this right passes to his or her personal representatives.

Rights of Partners

Under the Uniform Act, the second rank in order of payment is for those liabilities owed to partners other than for capital and profits. This provision is in accord with the general rule that in the absence of an agreement which will determine rights as to advances, each partner is a creditor of the firm as to money loaned it and has a right to repayment after the debts to other creditors have been met. The payment of interest on advances also falls within the second rank in order of payment if there is an express or implied agreement to pay interest.

The third rank in order of payment are those liabilities owed to partners in respect to capital. This is in accord with the general rule that after liability to third persons and firm debts to partners are paid, each partner is entitled to the repayment of the capital contributed by him or her. The fourth and last rank in order of payment are those liabilities owed to the partners in respect to profits. Each partner shall share equally in the profits and surplus remaining after all liabilities, including those to the partners, are satisfied. Unless there is an express or implied agreement to the contrary, the partners share equally in the profits, even though they may have contributed unequally to capital or services. The sharing of profits may be controlled by an express agreement between the parties, and an agreement may be implied from the course of conduct of the partners.

Rights of Separate Creditors

The Uniform Act provides that while partnership creditors have priority in regard to partnership assets, creditors of an individual partner have priority as to the individual property of that partner. Similarly, in applying the doctrine of marshalling assets the rule is recognized that creditors of the individual members of a partnership are entitled to preference over firm creditors in regard to the separate estates of the partners. The separate creditors may require firm creditors to exhaust their remedy against the firm before resorting to the property of its individual members. However, in some states, it has been held that after the partnership assets have been fully and fairly exhausted, partnership creditors are allowed to come in prorata with the separate creditors.

Death of a Partner

Unless the partners have previously agreed that dissolution would not occur, the death of a partner dissolves, by law, the partnership of which the deceased person was a member. The effect of death is to confer on the representatives of the deceased partner certain rights against the surviving partners and to impose upon the surviving partners certain corresponding obligations. The surviving partners and the representatives of the deceased partner may agree upon an adjustment of the partnership affairs upon any basis that they choose, and in the absence of mistake or fraud, this adjustment will be binding on all the parties to the agreement.

Glossary of Legal Terms

Acknowledgment
Formal declaration before authorized officials, by person who executed instrument, that it is his free act and deed.

Action
A suit or process at law; the procedure of instituting a law suit in a court of law.

Affidavit
A written declaration under oath; a statement of facts in writing signed by the party, and sworn to or confirmed by declaration before an authorized magistrate or notary public.

Ambiguous
Doubtfulness, doubleness of meaning; duplicity; indistinctness, or uncertainty of meaning of an expression used in written instrument. A want of clearness or definiteness; difficult to comprehend or distinguish; likely to be interpreted two ways; equivocal; indefinite.

Arbitrary
Given, adjudged, or done according to one's will or discretion; decided by an arbiter rather than by law; capricious; despotic; imperious; tyrannical; uncontrolled.

Arbitration
The act of arbitrating; the hearing and determination of a cause between parties in controversy, by a person or persons chosen by the parties.

Authorize

To give authority, warrant, or legal power to; to give a right to act; to empower; to make legal; to establish by authority or by usage or public opinion; to warrant; to sanction; to justify.

Bad Faith

The opposite of "good faith," generally implying or involving actual or constructive fraud, or a design to mislead or deceive another, or a neglect or refusal to fulfill some duty or some contractual obligation, not promoted by an honest mistake, or to one's rights or duties, but by some interest or sinister motive.

Bankrupt

Originally and strictly, a trader who secrets himself or does certain other acts tending to defraud his creditors. A person who has committed an act of bankruptcy; one who has done some act or suffered some act to be done in consequences of which, under the laws of his country, he is liable to be proceeded against by his creditors for the seizure and distribution among them of his entire property.

Bulk Sales Acts

A class of statutes designed to prevent the defrauding of creditors by secret sale in bulk of all or substantially all of a merchant's stock of goods.

Civil Law

"Civil Law," "Roman Law," and "Roman Civil Law" are convertible phrases, meaning the same system of jurisprudence. The system of jurisprudence held and administered in the Roman empire, particularly as set forth in the compilation of Justinian and his successors, and collectively called the "Corpus Juris Civilis" distinguishing it from the common law of England and the canon law.

Commerce

1. The exchange of goods, productions, or property of any kind. Intercourse by way of trade and traffic between different

peoples or states and the citizens or inhabitants thereof, including not only the purchase, sale and exchange of commodities, but also the instrumentalities and agencies by which it is promoted and the means and activities by which it is carried on, and the transportation of persons as well as of goods, both by land and by sea. 2. Internal commerce is that which is carried on between individuals within the same state, or between different parts of the same state. 3. Interstate commerce is that between states or nations entirely foreign to each other. 4. Intrastate commerce is that which is begun, carried on, and completed wholly within the limits of a single state, as contrasted with "interstate" commerce.

Commercial Law

A phrase used to designate the whole body of substantive jurisprudence applicable to the rights, intercourse, and relations of persons engaged in commerce, trade, or mercantile pursuits.

Commercial Paper

1. Bills of exchange, promissory notes, bank checks, and other negotiable instruments for the payment of money. Commercial paper is used to facilitate business transactions, as a substitute for the payment of money directly, and affords to the debtor an extension of time for the actual payment while offering certain protections and safeguards to all parties involved. 2. Basically, commercial paper includes negotiable and nonnegotiable promissory notes and negotiable and nonnegotiable drafts. See Article 3 of the Uniform Commercial Code.

Commingle

To mix together; to mingle in one mass; to blend.

Common Law

The general and ordinary law of a community receiving its binding force from universal reception. Historically, that body of law and juristic theory which was originated, developed, and formulated in England.

Company
A union of two or more persons for the carrying on of a joint enterprise or business.

Complaint
The first allegation made by a plaintiff in a civil lawsuit.

Consign
To deliver goods to a carrier to be transmitted to a designated factor or agent. To deliver or transfer as a charge or trust; to commit, in trust, give in trust, to transfer from oneself to the care of another; to send or transmit goods to a merchant, factor, or agent for sale; to deposit with another to be sold, disposed of, or called for.

Consignment
The act of process of consigning goods; the consigning of goods or cargo, especially to an agent for sale or custody; goods sent to a retailer who is expected to pay following sale.

Continuity
The state or quality of being continuous; a continuous or connected whole.

Contract
An oral, written, or implied agreement between two or more persons; an enforceable pact.

Construe
To arrange or combine, as words, syntactically; to analyze the grammatical construction of, as a sentence; to translate, especially orally; to show the meaning or intention of; interpret, as a law; put one's own interpretation on; to deduce by construction or interpretation; infer.

Corporation
A number of persons united or regarded as united in one body; an artificial person, created by law, or under authority of law, from a group or succession of natural persons, and having a continuous existence irrespective of that of its members, and powers and liabilities distinct from those of its members.

Default

Omission, neglect or failure of any party to take a step required of him in the progress of a case. When a defendant in an action at law omits to plead within the time allowed him for that purpose, or fails to appear at the trial, he is said to make default, and a judgment may be entered against him; it is called "judgment by default."

Doing Business

Within statutes on service of process on foreign corporation, equivalent to conducting or managing business. A foreign corporation is "doing business," making it amenable to process within a state, if it does business in the state in such a manner as to warrant the inference that it is present there—or that it has subjected itself to the jurisdiction and laws in which the service is made. The doing of business is the exercise in the state of some of the ordinary functions for which the corporation was organized. What constitutes doing business depends on the facts in each particular case, and the wording of the statute.

Domestic Corporation

A corporation incorporated under the laws of a state, as opposed to a foreign corporation formed under the laws of another state or nation.

Dormant Partner

A partner whose name is not used by the firm, and who is generally unknown to those dealing with the partnership.

Entity

A real being, existence.

Equitable

Possessing or exhibiting equity; equal in regard to the rights of persons; just; fair; impartial; pertaining to a court of equity.

Equitable Estoppel

That condition in which justice forbids one to gainsay his own acts or assertions. The preclusion of person by his act or conduct or silence from asserting rights which might otherwise have existed. The species of estoppel which equity put upon a person who has made a false representation or a concealment of material facts, with knowledge of the facts, to a party ignorant of the truth of the matter, with the intention that the other party should act upon it, and with the result that such party is actually induced to act upon it, to his damage.

Elements or essentials of such estoppel include change of position for the worse by party asserting estoppel.

Such estoppel may be based on acts, omissions to act, representations, admissions, concealment or silence.

Essential
Pertaining to, constituting, or entering into the essence or nature of a thing; important; fundamental; inherent; basic; absolutely necessary; indispensable; containing an essence of a plant or drug; something belonging to the essence or nature of a thing; something basic, necessary, a chief point.

Estoppel
A bar or impediment preventing one from asserting a fact or claim, arising from a previous action, or a failure to act, by which one has admitted, implied, or established a contrary position.

Fictitious
Feigned; not genuine, untrue. Of, or pertaining to fiction; dealing with imaginary characters and events.

Fiduciary
A person holding the character of a trustee, or a character analagous to that of a trustee, in respect to the trust and confidence involved in it and the scrupulous good faith and candor which it requires.

Fraud
An intentional perversion of truth for the purpose of inducing another, in reliance upon it, to part with some valuable thing belonging to him or to surrender a legal right; a false represen-

tation of a matter of fact, whether by words or by conduct, by false or misleading representations, or by concealment of that which should have been disclosed, which deceives, and is intended to deceive another so that he shall act upon it to his legal detriment.

Indemnity

A collateral contract or assurance, by which one person engages to secure another against an anticipated loss or to prevent him from being damaged by the legal consequences of an act or forebearance on the part of the parties or of some third person.

Independent Contractor

One who, in exercising an independent employment, contracts to do certain work according to his own methods, without being subject to the control of his employer, except as to the product or result of his work. The basic element of an independent contractor relationship is the fact that the contractor has an independent business or occupation. In general, it excludes the relation of principal and agent, master and servant, and the traditional employer-employee status.

Indicia

Signs; indications; circumstances which point to the existence of a given fact as probable, but not certain. For example, indicia of partnership are any circumstances which would induce the belief that a given person was in reality, though not ostensibly, a member of a given firm.

Individual Retirement Account (I.R.A.)

The Pension Reform Act of 1974, Employee Retirement Income Security Act or ERISA, contained a provision which permitted a new type of tax-favored retirement program (I.R.A.) for employees and self-employed persons who are not covered by a tax-qualified plan, government plan, or tax-sheltered annuity arrangement. Most insurance companies and savings and loan associations have various programs for these plans.

Joint Tenancy

Common ownership of property by two or more persons, with the property passing on to the surviving person or persons in case of the death of one coowner.

Joint Venture

An association of two or more persons to carry out a single business for profit which is usually, but not necessarily, limited to a single transaction.

Keogh Plan

Self-Employed Retirement Plans. (H.R. 10.) A self-employed participant can deduct the lesser of 15 percent of earned income or $7,500 per year.

Law Merchant

An expression substantially equivalent to the mercantile law or commercial law. It designates the system of rules, customs, and usages generally recognized and adopted by merchants and traders, and which, either in its simplicity or as modified by common law or statutes, constitutes the law for the regulation of their transactions and the solution of their controversies.

Liable

Answerable for consequences; under obligation legally to make good a loss; responsible; apt or likely to incur something undesirable; susceptible; subject or exposed to.

Limited Partnership

A partnership in which the liability of some members, but not all, is limited; such a partnership may be formed under most state statutes, which permit an individual to contribute a specific sum of money to the capital of the partnership and limit his liability for losses to that amount, upon the partnership complying with the requirements of the statute.

Litigation

The act or process of litigating; the proceedings in a suit at law; a lawsuit.

Misrepresentation

Any manifestation by words or other conduct by one person to another that, under the circumstances, amounts to an assertion not in accordance with the facts. An untrue statement of fact. An incorrect or false representation. That which, if accepted, leads the mind to an apprehension of a condition other and different from that which exists. False and fraudulent misrepresentation is a representation contrary to the fact, made by a person with a knowledge of its falsehood, and being the cause of the other party's entering into the contract. Negligent misrepresentation is a false representation made by a person who has no reasonable grounds for believing it to be true, though he does not know that it is untrue, or even believes it to be true.

Negotiable

Capable of being transferred by endorsement or delivery so as to pass to a holder the right to sue in his own name and take free of equities against the assignor.

Partnership

An association of two or more persons to carry on as coowners a business for profit.

Partnership at Risk Rule

Section 704(d) of the Internal Revenue Code, as amended by the Tax Reform Act of 1976, provides as follows: "(d) LIMITATION ON ALLOWANCE OF LOSSES. A partner's distributive share of partnership loss (including capital loss) shall be allowed only to the extent of the adjusted basis of such partner's interest in the partnership at the end of the partnership year in which such loss occurred. Any excess of such loss over such basis shall be allowed as a deduction at the end of the partnership year in which such excess is repaid to the partnership. For purposes of this subsection, the adjusted basis of any partner's interest in the partnership shall not include any portion of any partnership liability with respect to which the partner has no personal liability. The preceding sentence shall not apply with respect to any activity to the extent that Section 465 (relating to limiting deductions to amounts at risk in case of certain activities) applies, nor shall it apply to any partnership the principal activity of which is investing in real property (other than mineral property)."

Pension Reform Act of 1974; Employee Retirement Income Security Act of 1974 (ERISA)

1. An act which makes far-reaching changes in the entire area of pension, annuity, profit sharing, stock bonus, and employee welfare plans, in addition to broad structural and administrative changes. The statute requires pension plan fiduciaries to adhere to rigorous standards of fiduciary responsibility, imposes new restrictions for certain plan investments and penalizes specified prohibited transactions. It imposes detailed requirements for plan registration and requires disclosures relative to plan operations to the Internal Revenue Service, the Labor Department, and plan participants and their beneficiaries. 2. The act establishes a mandatory system of plan termination insurance for pension plans designed to protect participants against loss of benefits in the event the plan is terminated. Provision is made for a new type of tax-favored retirement program (I.R.A.) for employees and self-employed persons who are not covered by a tax-qualified plan, government plan, or tax-sheltered annuity arrangement.

Perpetual

Never ceasing; continuous; enduring; lasting; unlimited in respect of time; continuing without intermission or interval.

Piercing the Corporate Veil

In cases involving fraud or unjust enrichment, where the court refuses to recognize a corporation as an entity separate from those responsible for corporate activity, holding the corporation's alter ego liable, the court is said to pierce the corporate veil.

Plaintiff
A person who brings an action; the party who complains or sues in a personal action and is so named on the record.

Preponderance of Evidence
Greater weight of evidence, or evidence which is more credible and convincing to the mind. That which accords with reason and probability. The word preponderance means something more than weight; it denotes a superiority of weight, or outweighing. There is generally weight of evidence on each side in case of contested facts. But juries cannot properly act upon the weight of evidence, in favor of one having the onus, unless it overbears, in some degree, the weight upon the other side.

Priority
The state of being earlier in time, or of preceding something else; precedence in order, importance, or rank; the having of certain rights and privileges before another; that which needs or merits attention before others. When two persons have similar rights in respect of the same subject matter, but one is entitled to exercise his right to the exclusion of the other, he is said to have priority.

Pro Se
For himself; in his own behalf; in person. Usually used to designate a person who represents himself in a court case.

Process
In court practice, the means of compelling a defendant in an action to appear in court, generally, in civil actions, the service upon a defendant of a copy of the complaint and summons. If a defendant does not answer within a specified period of time (usually 20 to 30 days) a default may be entered against him.

Profits
Any advantage, benefit, or return; pecuniary gain; the advantage or gain resulting to the owner of capital from its employment in any undertaking; the excess of income over expenditure, specifically the difference, when an excess,

between the original cost and selling price of anything; the ratio in any year of this gain to the sum invested; revenue from investments or property.

Quasi
As if; almost as it were; analagous to.

Quorum
The numbers of persons, shares represented, or officers who may lawfully transact the business of a meeting.

Replevin
A court proceeding by which the owner, or one who has a property right in the chattel taken or detained, seeks to recover possession of that specific chattel; the recovery of damages or other relief is secondary to gaining possession of the thing.

Respondeat Superior
Let the master answer. This maxim means that a master is liable in certain cases for the wrongful acts of his servants and a principal for those of his agents.

Sale
A contract between a seller and a buyer, or purchaser, by which the seller, in consideration of the payment or promise of payment of a certain price in money, transfers to the purchaser the title and the possession of property.

Service of Process
The service of writs, summonses, rules, and other documents signifies the delivering to or leaving them with the party to whom or with whom they ought to be delivered or left; and, when they are so delivered, they are then said to have been served. Usually a copy only is served and the original is shown. Substituted service of process is accomplished by mailing a copy to the defendant and, in some instances publishing notice in a newspaper.

Shareholder
A person owning some part of the stock of a corporation.

Silent Partner

A partner whose connection with the partnership business is concealed and does not generally take any active part in the business.

Statute

An enactment of the legislative body of a government that is formally expressed and documented as a law; written, as opposed to common law. A permanent rule or law enacted by the governing body of a corporation or institution.

Statute of Frauds

This is the common designation of a very celebrated English statute (29 Car. II. C. 3) passed in 1677, and which has been adopted in a more or less modified form, in all states in this country. Its chief characteristic is the provision that no suit or action shall be maintained in certain classes of contracts or engagements unless there shall be a note or memorandum thereof in writing signed by the party to be charged or by his authorized agent. Its object was to close the door to the numerous frauds and perjuries.

Statute of Limitations

A statute imposing limits on the period during which certain rights, as the collection of debts, may be legally enforced.

Subscribe

To write, inscribe, or sign, as one's name, to a document, letter, or other paper; to express assent to, as a contract, by signing one's name; to attest to by signing, as a statement.

Subsequent

Following, coming, or being after something else in time; following in the order of place or succession.

Summons

A writ, directed to the sheriff or other proper officer, requiring him to notify the person named that an action has been commenced against him in the court whence the writ issues, and that he is required to appear, on a day named, and answer the complaint in such action.

Tort

A legal conception possessing the basic element of a wrong with resultant injury and consequential damage which is cognizable in a court of law. Actually, this is another word that the courts call "impossible" to define with precision. It is that great body of law described generally as a civil wrong— like a rap in the mouth (assault and battery) personal injury from auto accidents, libel and slander, malicious prosecution, and other personal types of hurt. The three elements of every tort action are:

1. existence of a legal duty from the defendant to the plaintiff;

2. breach of that duty; and

3. damage as a proximate result.

A legal wrong committed upon the person or property independent of contract. It may be either a direct invasion of some legal right of the individual, an infraction of some public duty by which special damage accrues to the individual or the violation of some private obligation by which damages accrue.

Trade Name

A name used in trade to designate a particular business of certain individuals considered somewhat as an entity, or the place at which a business is located, or of a class of goods, but which is not a technical trade mark either because not applied or affixed to goods sent into the market or because not capable of exclusive appropriation by anyone as a trademark. Trade names may, or may not, be exclusive.

Trustee

One to whom property or funds have been legally entrusted to be administered for the benefit of another; a person, usually one of a body of persons, appointed to administer the affairs of a company, institution, or the like.

Uniform Commercial Code
A code to regulate all aspects of commercial transactions, and accepted in all the states, except Louisiana.

Usury
An illegal contract for a loan or forbearance of money, goods, or things in action, by which illegal interest is reserved, or agreed to be reserved or taken. An unconscionable and exorbitant rate or amount of interest.

Valid
Sufficiently supported by actual fact; well grounded, sound, or just; good or effective; having sufficient legal strength or force; good or sufficient in point of law.

Validity
The state or quality of being valid; legal strength or force; soundness.

Void
Having no legal or binding force; null. Empty or not containing matter; vacant, unoccupied; devoid; destitute.

Waiver
An intentional relinquishment of a known right, interest, or advantage; an expression or written statement of such relinquishment.

Winding Up
The administration of assets for the purpose of terminating the business and discharging the obligations of the partnership to its members.

Writ of Attachment
A writ employed to enforce obedience to an order or judgment of the court. It may take the form of commanding the sheriff to attach the disobedient party and to have him before the court to answer his contempt.

A FREE ISSUE OF THE *CITIZEN'S LAW ADVISOR* IS WAITING FOR YOU!

Dear Friend,

Although this is the end of the book, it's just the beginning for you!

The *CITIZEN'S LAW ADVISOR* is a quarterly newspaper packed with human interest stories, advice on how readers are using the *CITIZEN'S LAW LIBRARY*, insights into tax shelters and other income sheltering and producing items, plus a complete book review and bookshelf section listing other titles in the field of layperson's law published by Prentice-Hall, Inc.

To receive your free complimentary issue of the *CITIZEN'S LAW ADVISOR* simply write your name and address on the coupon below and mail the coupon without further delay. Or call, toll-free, 1-800-228-2054 and tell the operator where you saw this announcement.

I look forward to hearing from you!

Sincerely yours,

J. Stephen Lanning

J. Stephen Lanning
Executive Vice President
Citizen's Law Library

CITIZENS LAW LIBRARY, Box 1745, 7 South Wirt Street, Leesburg, Va. 22075

Yes, please send me a free complimentary copy of the latest issue of THE CITIZENS LAW ADVISOR.

Signature _____

Name _____

Address _____

City _____ State _____ Zip _____

PYOPA